CANON WARS

CANON WARS

Whose Idea Was the Biblical Canon?

(A Response to Michael J. Kruger's
"7 Misconceptions" about the Biblical Canon)

Gary D. Collier, Ph.D.

⟁ The *Dialogē* Press
ἡ διαλογή

http://dialogepress.com
452 W Water St., Box 121,
Cloverdale, Indiana, 46120
Tuesday, August 13, 2024

Publisher's Cataloging-in-Publication Data

Names: Collier, Gary D., 1950-

Title: Canon wars : a response to Michael Kruger's "7 Misconceptions" about the Biblical canon / Gary D. Collier.

Description: Cloverdale, IN :, 2024. | Includes bibliographic references. | Summary: Reviews and responds to Michael Kruger's approach to the New Testament biblical canon, and offers an alternative.

Identifiers: LCCN 2024907966 | ISBN 9798991163101 (pbk.)

Subjects: LCSH: Kruger, Michael J. Canon revisited. | Bible. New Testament. | Bible. New Testament – Canon. | BISAC: RELIGION / Biblical Criticism & Interpretation / General. | RELIGION / Biblical Studies / General. | RELIGION / Biblical Commentary / New Testament / General.

Classification: LCC BS2320.C65 2024 | DDC 225.1'2 C--dc23

LC record available at https://lccn.loc.gov/2024907966

This printed version: Tuesday, August 13, 2024

Quotations from Old Testament and New Testament:

Unless otherwise indicated, all translations of Old or New Testament texts are by the author based on the following standard biblical texts: **New Testament:** *Novum Testamentum Graece*, Eberhard Nestle and Aland, Kurt (Eds.) 28th ed. (Stuttgart: Deutsche Bibelgesellschaft, 2013). **Old Testament:** *Biblia Hebraica Stuttgartensia* K. Elliger and W. Rudolph, (Eds.) (Stuttgart: Deutsche Bibelgesellschaft, 1977). Also *Septuaginta*, Alfred Rahlfs (Ed.)Deutsche Bibelgesellschaft Stuttgart, 1979.

To Lee Patmore

friend and conversation partner
in all things biblical text

Table of Contents

Introduction:

A YouTube video was posted on February 19, 2023, addressing "7 Misconceptions about Canon," by Dr. Michael Kruger,[1] president of Reformed Theological Seminary. Kruger has authored several books on the canon of the New Testament in which he argues that a New Testament book became *canonical* as soon as its ink dried, because God intended that book for the New Testament canon. Since God had made New Testament documents to be covenantally self-authenticating, the church's job was to *recognize* the books God had already chosen; the church most certainly did not *choose* the canon or make any book canonical.

In the video, Kruger dispels what he calls "7 Misconceptions" about the New Testament canon:

1. Early Christians who had heard about Jesus and heard the message of the Gospel did not even think there would be a new canon.

2. The authors of the New Testament did not think they were writing scripture.

3. Early Christians disagreed widely over which books belonged in the New Testament.

4. There was no canon until the fourth or fifth century.

5. Apocryphal books are just as valid as the New Testament books.

6. Apocryphal books were as popular as New Testament books.

---

[1] This was a live event for the Christ Covenant Church of Atlanta, GA. The video was posted under the title, "How did we get the Bible?" There was a second **live Q&A** video.

7. The New Testament books were picked by the church.

To be clear, Kruger disagrees with all of these.

I will say up front that I applaud Kruger's efforts in reworking and restating a defense of the classic Reformed view (in the lineage of B. B. Warfield) of the biblical canon: the best redrafting and redirecting of that classic defense to date. That said, I cannot count myself as a proponent either of that defense (although, in my youth and early training, I was inducted into a similar view), or of Kruger's revisions, or many of his conclusions; nor can I recommend them as the best options for the church at large or for individual Bible readers.

For my part, I think Kruger is fundamentally wrong and should not be followed on the question of canon. I do not accept that his approach and positions best represent the facts and claims of the biblical texts themselves. For that reason, I wish to distance myself from (and to critique) Kruger's representation of them. I hope my critique will be received as friendly, gracious, and fair, as well as reasonable, direct, and worthy of consideration.

The effort, here, is to offer a substantive response to Kruger's position as offered in the above mentioned speech, and including references to three of his books on canon. They will be noted as we get to them and are also listed on the final reference section.

As to the importance of this subject, I now wish to repeat the first words in my 2012 book, *Scripture, Canon, & Inspiration*, because I think they are every bit as relevant now as in 2012 when they were first penned:

> The Christian world is on the brink of a major shift in its view of the Bible. Many will not welcome this shift, and many are not aware that there is, right now, a raging conversation about it. This is no trivial conversation. . . . So, let us be clear from the start: the "origins and nature of the Bible" is not just a sensitive topic, it is potentially

explosive! It is often more a deeply rooted emotional issue than a carefully studied concern. And that emotion often lies just (barely) beneath the surface. (p. 14)

During the dozen years since that statement, *canon,* as a topic, has continued its climb into more popular venues. It is my hope that the present book can make some small contribution to the question. Chapters 1-5 are given to a pointed critique of Kruger's positions. I do, in fact, think there are legitimate and more proper ways to redirect the canon question, and chapters 6-10 are given to that.

I apologize in advance if there is any part of this book that comes across to Dr. Kruger or to anyone else as arrogant, unkind, or mean-spirited. I have worked hard to avoid any such voice, but I am aware that when offering critique, lines of sensitivity can move quite rapidly and without warning and can easily get crossed. My intention is to offer valid and reasonable critique and to suggest what I consider to be a better path, one that is more consistent with the biblical texts we call sacred.

Finally, I want to thank all of the members of the Scripture, Canon, & Inspiration Seminar of the *Institute for the Art of Biblical Conversation* (IABC) for their energetic pursuit of this topic during the 2023-24 seminar season, and for being true conversation partners. In particular, I want to mention Dr. Richard Davies, Lee Patmore, Dr. Brian Casey, Portia Regan, and Dr. Mike Wilkinson (who might or might not agree with the contents of this book on any particular matter) for reading and responding to numerous drafts of this book. Also I thank Lanette and Zoe for their patience and support as I worked on the manuscript. Naturally, I alone am responsible for what is stated here and for any failings this book might have.

Part I:
Review & Evaluation
of Kruger

–1–

The Concept & Meaning of Canon

Biblical texts (both Old and New Testaments) are among the most significant documents ever produced — if not, in fact, the most significant. To this day, they are crucial for the salvation of humankind from its own idiocy, its destructive trajectories, and its inclinations toward self-annihilation and horror.

Questions about, "Just what kind of book is the Bible?" persist. "What do we mean by *scripture*? What do we make of *canon*? And how do we evaluate the *inspiration* of those texts?"

Although such questions are often taken for granted, they are relevant generation after generation, and they are vital for healthy Christian individuals and communities. They are not merely questions for the eggheads among us; answers to them directly affect how we make decisions, how we act, and how we reach out to the tragedy that is humankind in the world. The entire 21st century church (not just biblical and theological scholars) should be energetically wrestling with these questions.

Such an engagement should be head on; not in *re*-action, but by *pro*-action; and not half-heartedly, but confidently in faith; not for tradition's sake alone, or for the sake of our pre-formed theological positions, or what sounds holy; not merely what is safe, or what will arouse the least ire among supporters. Our concerns about this topic must arise, instead, out of a dogged loyalty to the texts we say are sacred, and on the basis that we are acting with as much integrity with those texts as we can possibly muster.

I take Michael Kruger's 2023 speech on the canon of the Bible, along with his several books on the topic, as offered from such a desire. Even though I will now take serious issue with his approach, nothing I say here should be taken as a denigration of his motives, intentions, or even his effort in his works.

His speech in particular was offered in a "where-the-rubber-meets-the-road" type of popular venue. For that reason, I will use that speech as a doorway into responding to some of his key positions.

My approach will be as follows: I'll first offer 10 major concerns about his presentation (chapters 1-4). I'll turn, then, to give a short response to each of Kruger's listed "seven misconceptions" (chapter 5). From that point on, I'll offer an alternative that I believe would appropriately redirect discussion about canon and how we view "the Bible" in the world today (chapters 6-10).

Ten Concerns on Key Issues

I'll begin by looking at my first 3 concerns; namely, Kruger's presuppositions, his assertion that canon and canonical books are self-authenticating, and the meaning of the term *canon*.

Concern #1: Unstated & Underlying Presuppositions

The single biggest problem with Kruger's lecture is that it was compromised by three underlying and related assumptions:

1. **Assumption 1:** The biblical canon was God's idea from the start, and it was predetermined before any book was ever written;

2. **Assumption 2:** The concept of canon was understood, expected, and pursued, even by 1st century believers; and

3. **Assumption 3:** God's intended canon would culminate (eventually) in the current form of the canon that most Christians around the world now read.

These assumptions are widespread among many Bible readers, and Kruger uses that fact throughout his lecture. To be clear, he does not *argue* for these assumptions; he merely *makes* the assumptions and builds on them throughout his lecture as though they were ground-level facts.

Kruger would say that his books provide the foundation for the lecture (especially for number "2" above); but his books have the same problem, especially with numbers "1" and "3."

It may be helpful to remember that Kruger is the President of the Reformed Theological Seminary, and that in his books, he appeals to the approach of B. B. Warfield as a predecessor and as support for his own views.[2] So, it is most interesting that in the 1948 edition of Warfield's collected articles, Cornelius Van Til, who writes the Introduction, makes a telling comment about Warfield's views of the Bible:

> The view of Scripture as so ably presented and defended by Warfield is held by orthodox Protestants alone. And among these orthodox Protestants it is only the followers of Calvin who have a theology that fully fits in with this idea of Scripture. **Only a God who controls whatsoever comes to pass can offer to man His interpretation of the course of history in the form of an existential system. . . . [Arminians] have done and are doing excellent detail work in the defense of Scripture but they lack the theology that can give coherence to their effort .**[3]

The editor of the book, Samuel G. Craig, underscores the phrase "only the followers of Calvin," and then somewhat goads those

---

[2] See e.g., Kruger 2012, 75f; 2013, 41.

[3] Van Til, in Warfield 1948, 66f. Lit., " evangelical, that is a virtually Arminian."

of the Lutheran or Arminian theological persuasions that they would have to show how Warfield's conception of Scripture, "fits into, finds a more natural and logical a place in their systems of theological thought . . . than in the Reformed."[4]

To whatever degree Kruger would accept such direct and exclusive language, he all but demonstrates the same approach by identifying two main, what he calls, *definitions* for the pursuit of canon, and then adding a third:

1. The **exclusive** definition (i.e., historical). This approach claims there was no canon until the 4th century when it was finally completed; and

2. the **functional** definition (i.e., tradition-historical). This approach claims that *canon* was a process that developed over time and that can be traced through intertextual processes. Finally, to these he adds a third approach:

3. the **ontological** definition (i.e., theologically pre-determined). This approach claims that *canon* was in the mind of God from the start, and is God-ordained. It happens (or becomes a reality) as soon as a document is written and before the ink is dry on the page. The only job of the church is to discover which books of the canon God had already given.

Kruger does not accept that either of the first two is sufficient on its own (and he especially rejects the exclusivist nature of the first). The third, he says, is a necessary addition, and they all complement each other: "all three should be used in an integrative and multidimensional manner." [5] The biggest question Kruger

---

[4] No page is listed, but this is the 3rd (and final) page of the Foreword.

[5] Kruger 2012 chapter 2; the quote on p. 42; see also p. 280 for the difference between a *closed* and *settled* canon; and 2013, chapter 1. The phrase, "Before the ink is dry," is in the public lecture.

tries to answer is this: how can we, as Christians, "know that we have the right 27-books in our New Testament?"[6]

Kruger is unapologetic that his approach (the ontological definition) is intentionally theological, rather than historical or textual; and he acknowledges that his view won't be accepted by "the broader world of critical scholarship" because "it will be criticized as question begging or irrelevant theologizing."[7]

In fact, Kruger's approach is exactly that: a blatant form of **theological anachronism** (a reading into an earlier time understandings or sensibilities of a later time)[8]; and yes, it actually does **beg the question:** it theologically assumes as true what one is attempting to prove.[9] This is a huge problem that undermines Kruger's entire argument, turning historical and tradition-historical approaches into theological lapdogs.

Concern #2: Supernatural Selection & Self-Authorizing Texts

This makes it easier, then, to understand that when Kruger speaks of "normal historical channels," he is doing more than repeating a common trope for how the church selected the canon:

> The canon was put together by God . . . in his providence for his own reasons through normal historical channels.

---

[6] Kruger 2012, 15.

[7] Kruger 2012, 294. See also pp. 23 and 67ff.

[8] Anachronism has been a concern in canon studies for a long time (at least since 1968 when Barton said *canon* was anachronistically applied to Old Testament). But Chapman 2012 and others have pushed back, rejecting that terms like *Bible, canon,* and *scripture* should not be used, and maintaining that the concept of canon could exist even before a set of books were a reality. I reject this, since, in theory canon is defined one way, but then in fact, canon gets applied with later canonical awareness or sensitivities. Kruger routinely does this. It is inappropriate.

[9] This is the formal definition of "begging the question" in logic: "Aristotle's phrase *petitio principii* means 'assume the conclusion,'" and is "used to name the logical fallacy in which an argument assumes the very thing it's trying to prove." Merriam-Webster online.

> Somebody had to sit down with a quill and write it; then it had to get copied by scribes; then it had to be carried by a letter carrier to another part of the empire.[10]

This is not a common trope about a natural selection process; for Kruger, the church did not *select* a canon; it merely *recognized* what God had already decided and ordained—we might say, *"canon by supernatural selection."* These are my words, but this is a view found in conservative works for nearly a century and a half, taking shape essentially in Warfield's (1892) development of the view of verbal plenary inspiration, and explicitly restated in works like Tenney (1953) and Packer (1965).[11] The end result, says Kruger, is that the canon is self-authenticating.

By *self-authenticating* he means that "the canon itself provides the necessary direction and guidance for how it is to be authenticated." Indeed, one cannot "authenticate the canon without appealing to the canon." And this means that the church

1. must first *receive* a canonical book;

2. *recognize* (a) its divine qualities, (b) its reception by the church as a whole, and (c) its apostolic origins;

---

[10] Kruger 2023, at 29:22.

[11] Warfield stated this without the words *determined* or *recognized*: "[T]he Christian church did not require to form for itself the idea of a ' canon,' — or, as we should more commonly call it, of a ' Bible,' — that is, of a collection of books given of God to be the authoritative rule of faith and practice. It inherited this idea from the Jewish church, along with the thing itself, the Jewish Scriptures, or the ' Canon of the Old Testament.' The church did not grow up by natural law: it was founded. And the authoritative teachers sent forth by Christ to found His church, carried with them, as their most precious possession, a body of divine Scriptures, which they imposed on the church that they founded as its code of law. No reader of the New Testament can need proof of this; on every page of that book is spread the evidence that from the very beginning the Old Testament was as cordially recognized as law by the Christian as by the Jew. The Christian church thus was never without a ' Bible ' or a ' canon.'" See also Tenney 1953, 405 "The church did not *determine* the canon; it *recognized* the canon" (emphasis his); Packer 1965, "The church no more gave us the New Testament canon than Sir Isaac Newton gave us the force of gravity."

3. and have this process verified by the internal testimony of the Holy Spirit.[12]

Kruger admits and defends the circular nature of his argument,[13] which, in my opinion, is essentially, if we can assume a canon, we can bathe it in enough theological language it to say that the canon itself, defends itself. Why this exact process could not be used to defend any canon of any size and shape is apparently because it would not fit the assumptions and parameters of Kruger's Reformed theology.

By *canon*, Kruger continually assumes the version of the Old/New Testament Protestant canon we have today, and he also assumes and implies that *the whole, completed canon — as a canon —*itself was inspired, not just the individual letters and books themselves.[14]

Of course, the reasoning is circular and at least a bit audacious: we assume our own canon, and then use it to prove that God has given us the one, true, "self-authenticating" canon. Lampooning this approach, Bird and Wright recast it in terms of Indiana Jones:

> . . . there are many who, taught to "believe the Bible," treat the New Testament canon as a self-evident and self-authorizing collection. For them, it would only be a slight caricature to say that the church Fathers, like early versions of Indiana Jones, went searching for "scriptures," finding hidden scrolls in ancient catacombs or sneaking into imperial palaces to steal confiscated copies of the gospels. Then, equipped with some kind of magic device for telling which documents were "inspired," they added their freshly

---

[12] This is not brought out in the videos, but is laid out in Kruger 2012, 91-122, in the chapter, "My Sheep Hear My Voice: Canon as Self-Authenticating." The quote above are from pp. 91 and

[13] Kruger 2012, 91ff.

[14] Kruger 2012, 152ff for Old Testament canon. He tends to bounce over the top of those who point out the unfinished nature of canon in the first century.

discovered texts to their collection of what became "Holy Scriptures."[15]

Concern #3: The Meaning of Canon

To take this further, the issues at stake are fundamental for how Christians view the Bible. Many see discussions about canon as a game of trivial pursuit—as marginally interesting, but ultimately, as little more than academic tidbits about "how we got the Bible." So, here are some facts that need to be understood:

1. Christians of the 1st century never used the term *canon* to describe their holy texts, documents, or scrolls—not ever.

2. In fact, it wasn't used for that purpose until about 320 or so years after the first New Testament document was written, when Athanasius of Alexandria (in 367 CE) "set forth in order the books that are canonized (*kanonizomena*), transmitted, and believed to be divine"[16] in the service of combating false teaching.

3. Even so, it would be 1,400 more years before the word *canon* gets pulled into service for a closed collection of "selected books" in classical literature. Rudolf Pfeiffer writes in his *History of Classical Scholarship from the Beginnings to the End of the Hellenistic Age*:

    > "In the year CE 1768 the term "canon" was coined for them by David Ruhnken when he

---

[15] Bird & Wright 2019, 867. In addition to the Indiana Jones analogy, Kruger's self-authorizing proof might also be compared to the "Fani Willis" defense: "The proof is what I just told you." Only, here, biblical texts don't even *tell us* such a thing.

[16] Text and translation from Gallagher/Mead 2017, 121f. The full quote is: "I have been urged by genuine brothers and sisters and instructed from the beginning, to set forth in order the books that are canonized (*kanonizomena*), transmitted, and believed to be divine, so that those who have been deceived might condemn the person who led them astray."

> wrote: Ex magna oratorum copia tamquam in
> canonem decem dumtaxat rettulerunt . . .
> [From a great number of orators, as if they
> brought ten into the canon]. . . His coinage met
> with worldwide and lasting success, as the
> term was found to be so convenient; one has
> the impression that most people who use it be-
> lieve that this usage is of Greek origin. But
> *kanōn* was never used in this sense, nor would
> this have been possible. From its frequent use
> in ethics *kanōn* always retained the meaning of
> rule or model."[17]

4. Since the 18th century, biblical scholars have struggled to define the word *canon*. Does it refer (a) to a canonical process that leads to a final canon? Or (b) only to a final, fixed, closed canon? (c) Should we speak of canon 1, 2, or 3?[18]

5. Kruger, offers an end-run around this debate with an updated version of the traditional B. B. Warfield[19] approach, what Kruger calls "the ontological definition"[20] of canon, meaning that every document intended by God for the canon is intrinsically, in its very being, (i) inspired, (ii) Scripture, (iii) and canon—all three at once, as soon as the ink dries, whether anyone knows it or not.

6. This approach both draws upon and feeds into the widespread current-day view of (or assumption about) the

---

[17] See also McDonald/Sanders, 2002, 11-13; and McDonald 2007, 51f, 307.

[18] Naturally, this debate is much more involved. McDonald 2007, 55 summarizes how the debate becomes formalized as **Canon 1**: "an authoritative voice in written or oral form that was read and received as having the authority of God in it"; **Canon 2**: "a perpetual fixation or standardization, namely, when the books of the Bible were fixed or stabilized." See also Kruger 2013, 29-40.

[19] As Kruger makes clear on p. 41.

[20] Kruger 2013, 40.

Bible that the very word *canon* means **the specific group of books that God intended to give to his people: the Bible.** As such, the word *canon* is interchangeable with other words, like *Bible, Scripture, inspired,* and the like.

All of this together explains why many are stunned when they're asked this next question: **"Whose idea was canon in the first place?"** They're understandably stumped (and maybe shocked, unsettled, or angry) when they realize that *no biblical text ever claims that God had in mind all along—or at any point—to give a specific "inspired canon" of books to be called "the Bible."*

However, Kruger is not at all bothered by such a question or reality because (1) he overtly conflates the words *canon* and *scripture*,[21] so that they mean essentially the same thing; and (2) he thinks we are ultimately rescued from that dilemma by invoking the concept of covenant (which I'll get to in another chapter). It's important to realize that in Kruger's presentation, when he says canon, he is assuming (eventually) the current-day version of the Protestant canon. As a result, he treats books in the New Testament one way, and books in the Apocrypha another way.

As an example: Paul's letters are said to get recognized as canon by 2Peter 3 (because that text uses the word *graphē*,[22] and even though canon is not used); whereas Jude is simply quoting 1Enoch as a helpful book. Again, notice that by introducing the word canon into a time it was not even used, this also introduces later theology and attitudes about a so-called, "God-intended" canon.

There is much more to this, but my point at the moment is that the word canon is a loaded term. (a) It was not used by 1st century

---

[21] Kruger 2013, 31-32, argues very weakly for this. He never (that I could find) deals with the fact that no biblical document says one thing about canon.

[22] *graphē* is usually translated "Scripture" in the New Testament. Kruger 2013, 33, uses this as a basis for conflating *scripture* and *canon*. See my challenge below pp. 19ff.

Christians for their books, (b) not all today mean the same things by it, and (c) these facts make it not only possible, but likely, that those using it today to describe what the earliest Christians thought will (subtly or overtly) read current conceptions anachronistically onto and into biblical texts.

In chapter 2, I'll proceed to my concern #4: Canon, Authority, and Collections of Books.

–2–

Canon, Authority, & Collections

This chapter will focus entirely on . . .

Concern #4: Canon, Authority, & Collections

a. Authority or Canon?

In his speech, Kruger equates the word *authority* with the word *canon*, as though one is interchangeable with the other. He readily runs back and forth, vacillating between the two words. This is little more than a muddling of terminology.[23] More than once, Kruger finds something about *authority* in a New Testament document, and then he treats it as a claim, or a proof, or an indication of *canonicity*. He then extends this supposed claim to all New Testament documents, across the board, as if what's true for one must be true for all. The best example of this is when he quotes 1Cor 14:37:

> If anyone thinks that he is a prophet, or spiritual, he should acknowledge that what I am writing to you is a command of the Lord.[24]

---

[23] I pointed to this fallacy of *conflation* or *interchangeability of terms* in Collier 2012, 87f.

[24] Kruger 2023 at 21:10.

Kruger says Paul's claim to writing this "command of the Lord" is a claim to canonicity of the whole letter of 1Corinthians. In his words: "As soon as the ink is dry on the page, it already bears authority from the outset."[25]   So then, from the moment a New Testament document was written, it was authoritative, which, for Kruger, means it was *canonical*, and this extends to all New Testament documents.

Kruger makes these interchangeable associations throughout, and he applies them even to collections of books. He says he means *authority* when he says, "canon," but he easily slips from the word *authority* to a list of books—for example, in these words:

> I think Christianity was the exact perfect theological soil, if you will, out of which **a new canon would sprout**. Yes, they already had **an Old Testament canon. . . .**[26]

The phrases "a new canon would sprout" and "an Old Testament canon" are clearly referring to a list or set number of books which, for Kruger, God intended and were predetermined.

The problem is not insignificant or merely subtle. When words like *authority, canon, Scripture,* and *Bible,* are used in such a slippery fashion, so that one can be used for the other, then the individual words mean nothing in themselves, except what the underlying theological perspective needs them to mean in any given situation.

b. Canon or Collections?

Kruger does not distinguish between a *canon* and a *collection.* He uses these phrases:

❖ a new collection of books
❖ a new written collection of books

---

[25] Kruger 2023 at 20:23.

[26] Kruger 2023, at 11:34.

❖ a reliable collection of New Testament books

Not one of these phrases is objectionable *per se*. Even so, it is one thing to talk about collections of documents; it is another thing to start calling that collection a *canon* (when those writers did not) and to say or assume that we know exactly what was in those collections, or how tight or loose those collections were, or even how comparatively authoritative we assume them to be. I will turn now to two specific examples.

c. 2Pt 3:16 and "The Letters of Paul"

> . . . just as also our beloved brother *Paul*, in keeping with the wisdom given to him, wrote to you, as also *in all his letters*, speaking about these things, in which are some hard-to-understand things which the ignorant and unstable distort as also the rest of the writings to their own destruction.

(1) When 2Pt 3:16 says in passing: "all his letters," *what, exactly, did that include?* Kruger appears to build on the assumption that his own hearers today will naturally (and in his view, appropriately) think of the 13 letters of Paul we have today and then conclude, "Ah, this is the New Testament showing us how God is bringing the canon into existence."

But the notion of 13 letters is an assumption.[27] Maybe this was only a specific group of letters, like Galatians, Ephesians, and Colossians. Or maybe v 15 gives a clue when it says, "forbearance . . . in **all** his letters" and includes only the letters of Paul that talk about forbearance/patience.[28] How about the letter to the

---

[27] In the Q&A, Kruger was asked whether, if a new letter of Paul was discovered and widely accepted as genuine today, it should be added to the canon. His answer was no, because the canon is closed. His position forces him to this answer, since our current form of the Protestant canon is the inspired canon intended by God. A new book would present a breach of the canon.

[28] The most immediate guess one might make is from the context of 2Pt 3:15f: "And count the **forbearance** of our Lord as salvation. So . . . Paul wrote to you . . . in **all his letters**." Forbearance *makrothumia* occurs in these Pauline texts: Rom 2:4; 9:22; 2Cor

Laodiceans ("see that you read also the letter from Laodicea" Col. 4:16)? Was that in their collection?[29] Or how about Hebrews? It talks about forbearance.[30] Did 2Peter think that was written by Paul, if it indeed existed at that time? Or maybe 2Peter meant just any letter by Paul that he might write. The point is, there is no direct and decisive way to know what was in this collection of letters in 2Pt 3:16. This letter makes only a general statement about this collection—and it is *in passing*. It doesn't give specifics, and we don't know the specifics.[31]

(2) Furthermore, *what is the main point of this text?* Kruger focuses on the word *Scripture* as proof for canonicity, which again, shows the muddling of two words. However, when 2Pt 3:16 mentions "all his letters" alongside "the rest of the writings," his point is not,

> Hey, guys! Paul's letters are **Scripture**!
> That means that Paul's writings are equal to the **Torah**!

Maybe *we* want it to say that, but his point is how people twist the difficult parts of Paul's letters to their own destruction. For all we know, it might be like what readers will say about me when finished here:

> Collier twists what Kruger says just like he does all the other texts he looks at!

6:6; Gal 5:22; Eph 4:2; Col 1:11; 3:12; 1Tim 1:16; 2Tim 3:10; 4:2. Only Romans and 1Timothy speak about the forbearance of the Lord. If one suggests that "all" is a generalized "all," meaning actually "most of his letters," then maybe *graphē* is a generalized use which means merely "other writings." Naturally, none of this is decisive, and critical commentaries explore possibilities.

[29] Since that letter was recommended by Paul (Col 4:16), would that imply it was as important to him as Colossians? In the Q&A Kruger said that even if the letter to the Laodiceans referred to in Colossians was discovered and verified, it would not be canonical. The canon is set. (Presumably, God would not allow one of his intended canonical books to be lost.) This is an example of a theory about inspiration and canon overriding and discounting a plain statement in a text.

[30] Heb 6:12 "imitate those who through faith and forbearance inherit the promises."

[31] Such things are discussed in critical studies.

It is not true that the phrase *tas loipas* ("the others, the rest") must imply that Paul's letters are just like "the other writings," whatever they are. This can easily be shown. Luke 24:9 uses the same word, when it says this

> ... once the women returned from the tomb, they reported all these things to the eleven *and to all the others.*

When this text says, "To all the *others*," everyone understands that it simply means, "and to everybody else who was there." No one would claim that "the others" in this text, would need to be exactly like the eleven in all respects — or in *any* respect, for that matter. If that were the case, that kind of clarification or emphasis would need to be provided by other words in the context.

The same thing is true in 2Peter 3. If the point is to say, "Hey, Paul's letters are equal to the law and the prophets," the context would need to be much more specific. Kruger, of course, would say, "Aha! But it *is* more specific!" He points to the Greek word *graphē* (usually translated "Scripture" in this text) and says it implies *canon.*

For example, in his 2013 book, Kruger asks, "Must we make a sharp distinction between the definitions of *scripture* and *canon?*"[32] His answer is "No!" This way, he gets to abduct any occurrence of the word *graphē* as "scripture," and make it mean "canon." Once again, Kruger's penchant for mashing words together to mean the same thing raises its head.

Kruger is not alone in this huge assumption and faulty equation; a large majority of interpreters see the word *graphē* as a specialized term in the New Testament that should be translated *Scripture.*

But I have challenged this. I have offered a comprehensive word study of every occurrence of the word *graphē* in biblical and

---

[32] Kruger 2013, 27ff is subtitled: "Must we make a sharp distinction between the definitions of scripture and canon?

related texts. In 2018 (2nd edition 2024), I published the book *Graphē in Biblical and Related Literature*. It's subtitle is, "Is the term *scripture* an appropriate translation in English Bibles?" The following is from the conclusion:

> ***A more accurate and contextually sensitive layout of the usage of*** γραφή | ***graphē in biblical and related literature has been set forth.*** Specifically, the word γραφή | *graphē* is used (1) *in the singular definite* in all of our literature to point to all kinds of individual texts, verses, quotations, or documents; and (2) *in the plural* when pointing to an *undefined plurality* of documents. Throughout this study, the reference to an "undefined plural" has never meant that we have no idea what any of the texts might have been, as if they might have been random texts from hither and yon. Rather, the point is that, *whether singular or plural, the word* γραφή | *graphē always depends on its context for help in such things. That is to say, the word itself does not make any comment about whether the writings are either (a) sacred writings, or (b) some imaginary canon. If there is anything to be said about the* **inherent nature** *of texts being referred to, or about their* **limits or boundaries**, *that will be provided by the context and not by the word* γραφή | *graphē itself.*[33]

Just because many (today) routinely translate the word *graphē* as *Scripture* (usually, with a capital 'S'), and then equate Paul's letters with "the other Scriptures," it's a mistake to put all of our weight on this word and then jump to *canonicity*.

As a corroboration of what I'm saying, compare Bauckham's comment in 1983, when he says about 2nd Peter 3:16:

---

[33] Collier 2024, 143. Bold and italics are original to the quote.

> *Graphē* was not limited to the books of the Old Testament canon, but could be used for apocryphal writings. It need not therefore imply a *canon* of Scripture at all." [34]

Clearly, 2Pt 3:16 contextually implies that an undefined plurality of Paul's letters deserve special attention by believers as they await the Lord. Whether that collection would have been viewed as "equal to the Torah" is at least open to question (not to mention whether Paul would have agreed with it). The author gives no attention or detail about how weighty he thinks they are in comparison to the other writings mentioned. Nor does he say or imply, "We have now added Paul's collected letters (however many there were) to our new-covenant canon!" It is easy to see how Kruger can read his views of *canon/authority/inspiration/Scripture* into this text; but there is nothing about this text that helps us to arrive naturally at his presuppositional view. When such a theological presupposition drives the interpretation, anything can happen.

(3) Finally, for 2Pt 3:16, it is not clear at all *when this was made*, or even *how widespread* it was. Of all the New Testament documents, 2Peter had the latest and least support to be included in the canon of the Western church. The Roman Catholic New Testament scholar, Raymond Brown, wrote about this letter:

> In the Western church (unlike Jude) II Peter was either unknown or ignored until ca. 350, and even after that, Jerome reported that many rejected it because it differed in style from I Peter.[35]

---

[34] Bauckham 1983, 333. He lists as examples: Jas 4:5; Barn. 16:5; 1Clem. 23:3; cf. Herm. Vis. 2:3:4 ὡς γέγραπται [*hōs gegraptai*], "as it is written."

[35] Brown 1997, 769. See also Donald A. Hagner 2012, 722; and Gallagher/Mead 2017, 278, "Origen [d. 253, gdc] is the first extant author to mention Peter's second epistle." Quite naturally, some have expressed the possibility that 2Peter was written in Peter's name, in part, to clear up the rift that Paul speaks about in Galatians.

2Peter is not listed in the controversial Muratorian fragment,[36] which Kruger insists is a late 2nd century document. Unfazed by such concerns, Kruger gives 2Peter unfettered weight as the key text for proving that the letters of Paul *were regarded as Scripture, and therefore as canon*—and at an early date.

The point here is not that 2Peter should be disregarded; the point is that we should be more careful as responsible readers. Even if this letter were regarded as written in the 60's-80's, it is impossible to know how influential it was, or in what circles; or whether the Jewish-Christian communities of, say, Matthew, or James, or Jude shared such a high view of Paul. (Perhaps they did. But there is no way to tell this just by reading 2Peter.)[37]

What if the letter were written in the 2nd century? (Say, 120 to 140 CE?) If so, then it could have been an effort to smooth over any leftover notions of a rift between Peter and Paul.

Whatever the case, and regardless of the date, this letter does not reflect any specific content in Paul's letters (beyond his reference to "the forbearance of the Lord"). So, there is no substantial internal evidence in 2Peter for which of Paul's letters might have been intended.

To summarize: Responsible readers will want to be careful not to overread what is stated in 2Peter 3:16. First, we cannot be sure about it's date, location, or even it's authorship. Second, we must take seriously (a) that the letter was slow to be accepted into the canon, and (b) that it did so only very late in the process.

A big problem with respect to Kruger's claims about 2Peter 3:16 is that he overreads the text with his free-running, overlapping, and interchangeable use of terms like *canon, authority,* and

---

[36] Gallagher/Mead 2017, 182.

[37] Bauckham 1983,157, thinks 2Peter was written in the 80's or 90s, but notes that "No book in the New Testament has been assigned such a wide range of dates as 2Peter," which scholars have put "in every decade from 60 to 160 CE"—except in the 70s.

collections. In doing so, he makes this text claim or imply things about canon that it does not actually claim or imply.

d. Luke 24 and Jude

A second example: Since, theoretically, *canon* equals *authority* for Kruger, would that earliest canon include the Assumption of Moses and 1Enoch? Jude 1:9 alludes to these books as authoritative, and 1:14 directly quotes 1Enoch for *his* community of believers.[38] Now, just who was Jude? He was the brother of Jesus and of James the Just, leader of the Jerusalem church. So, this is important: *1Enoch is treated by Jude as sacred and authoritative* — just like Paul quotes Jeremiah, or like Jesus quotes Isaiah or refers to the law and the prophets. Furthermore, Jude is far more specific about the authoritative, prophetic nature of 1Enoch than 2Peter is about Paul's letters.

So then, since Kruger views authoritative books as "canon," then one might think that he would feel at least somewhat comfortable translating Lk 24:44 this way:

> These are my words which I spoke to you, while I was still with you, that everything written about me *in the canon* must be fulfilled.

However, even if he would agree to that in Luke, Kruger would not agree to applying this very same standard to Jude 14. He would, in fact, object if one were to translate Jude 14 like a Christian targum (i.e., an expansive paraphrase), so that it would read like this:

> As Enoch the seventh from Adam (a book in our *canon* that preceded the time of Moses) *prophesied . . .*

Kruger would not accept this. He would object specifically that the word *graphē* is not used here, which means that Jude was

---

[38] Bauckham thinks Jude was written in the 50's, but possibly as late as the 80's. If in the 50's, a full generation before 2Peter.

not claiming this as *Scripture* and therefore not as *canon*. How do we know Kruger would do this? Because he states it specifically in the Q&A of his speech in the following words:

> 1Enoch gives us information that is helpful and Jude quotes it interestingly. You may know when you read the book of Jude, [that] actually Jude refers to 1Enoch and uses it. He doesn't quote it as Scripture but he does refer to it as useful and valuable, and so that's another example of how outside books can still be utilized as helpful but not as scriptural.[39]

The problem is, Kruger is incorrect in what he says. He gives a common misapplication of the term *graphē* in the New Testament with the result that he dismisses Jude 14. In my book on this topic, *Graphē in Biblical and Related Literature,* I talk specifically about how the word *graphē* is used in the New Testament. Note the following:

> It is a mistake to think that all uses of *graphē* in the New Testament are the same. The general New Testament pattern is as follows: (1) it has an article; (2) in the singular it refers to a specific verse, text, or book; (3) in the plural it refers to more than one book or to one or more collections (like 'law' and/or 'prophets'). Never do New Testament authors use the singular to say, "Scripture says," referring to "Scripture as a whole."[40]

But to the larger point: Like Jude, the book of Hebrews *also* never uses the term *graphē*.[41] Does that mean that, like Jude, the writer of Hebrews considered all the texts he quoted as useful, but not as *Scripture*? Kruger simply offers an improper evaluation of such texts. In the process, he unintentionally shows why it's a mistake

---

[39] Kruger 2023 Q&A at 15:40.

[40] See Collier 2024, 64, where I'm specifically challenging many statements to the contrary. This is fully developed and argued, and a specific critique is given of BDAG's flawed entry on the word.

[41] The single occurrence of the perfect tense verb *gegraptai* "it is written" in the quote from Ps 40 (based on Jer 36:2) does not contradict this fact.

both to apply later terms to earlier texts, and to use *Scripture* and *canon* interchangeably.

Now back to Lk 24:44: if Law/Prophets/Psalms are *canon* for Jesus, then why is 1Enoch not *canon* for his brother? (Even the Dead Sea Scrolls considered 1Enoch as authoritative.) The fact is, calling either of these canon is not appropriate. The big issue here is that of *anachronism*. When we apply later terms anachronistically to earlier times, we start reading our preconceptions about that later term into those earlier texts. The term *canon* is not appropriate for either of these scenarios.

Up to this point, I have discussed four of my ten concerns about Kruger's speech. In the next chapter—chapter 3—I'll look at four more concerns: the first two about Scripture and early Christians; the last two about covenants.

— 3 —

Scripture, Early Christians,
& Covenants

This chapter will focus on concerns 5-8.

Concern #5: The Nature of *Scripture* vs the Apocrypha

Kruger says New Testament texts never quote the Apocrypha *as Scripture*:

> Our New Testament authors—Paul, Peter, John: the Gospel authors, including Jesus, within those—cite the Old Testament hundreds and hundreds of times. Not a single time, ever, do they cite a book from the Apocrypha as Scripture. Not even once. [42]

The key words here are *as Scripture*. Kruger is relying on two things for this conclusion: (a) from the start, by the word *canon* he assumes our current modified Protestant canon. So, if the Apocrypha is quoted or alluded to at all, he says it is not *as Scripture*; and as further proof, (b) he says the word *graphē* is not applied to them in New Testament writings. But this, too, is both misleading and one-sided.

---

[42] Kruger 2023 Q&A at1:30.

1. His focus on the word "Scripture" is misleading: It's a methodological fallacy to *assume* the canon you want and then judge everything from that. This is, again, a misuse of the word *graphē*, and it is a common misuse in English translations. A quick example will suffice:

James 2:23 (quoting Gen 15:6) is almost always translated as

> The ***Scripture*** [*graphē*] was fulfilled. . . .

But when the exact same Greek wording refers to a pseudepigraphical book, it is typically translated not as *Scripture*, but merely as *writing* or *book*. Note three different pseudepigraphical books,[43] all referring to the book of Enoch, to see how the translators handle the terms:

graphēs Henōch	"the ***writing/book*** of Enoch"[44]
en graphēi nomou Henōch	"in the ***book*** of the law of Enoch"[45]
en graphēi hagiai Henōch	"in the holy ***writing*** of Enoch"[46]

The Greek is the same as James 2:23. However, the *translation* is based, not on the widespread usage of the word, but on canonical assumptions. James gets special treatment because James and Genesis are in our current canon. Unfortunately, this is common practice. It is simply misleading and inappropriate to make the claim that New Testament writers do not regard books other than the "Old Testament" as inspired.[47]

2. His focus on the word "Scripture" is also one-sided. Namely, using the occurrence (in 2Pt 3:16) or absence (in Jude 1:14) of the

---

[43]The following texts are discussed fully in Collier 2024, 56 and 155. I list, now, only three examples from among many others.

[44] T. Sim 5:4; T. Levi 14:1

[45] T. Zeb 3:4. This text begins with *gegraptai* "it is written."

[46] T. Naph 4:1.

[47] See 67 pages of quotations, allusions, and similarities with apocryphal/pseudepigraphical literature in the New Testament: Evans 2005, 342-4-09, and the abbreviated 13 pages in McDonald 2007, 552-64.

word "Scripture" to show whether writers of New Testament documents thought a writing was inspired is not a legitimate test. This is easy to demonstrate. For example:

a. These 14 New Testament "books" **never use the term** *graphē*: [48]

2Corinthians	1-2Thessalonians	Hebrews
Ephesians	Titus	123John
Philippians	Philemon	Jude
Colossians		Revelation

Would this mean that they don't consider any of their quoted texts as *inspired*, just because they don't use the word usually translated as "Scripture"? Since that is obviously ludicrous, the real reason Jude's direct quote of 1Enoch is denied "inspired status" by Kruger is a one-sided, predetermined canon prejudice that is read back onto Jude.[49]

b. There are 10 New Testament "books" that **never directly quote** any Old Testament text, and the three in bold don't even make *allusions* to the Old Testament:

---

[48] 2Cor 8:15; 9:9; Heb 10:7; and Rev 13:8 all have the form *gegraptai* ("it is written"), and this word is often claimed by current authors to prove "Scripture" in the same way as the noun *graphē* is cited. But even a fast study of this form shows it is used of numerous books not in our current canon. Key among these are the numerous books mentioned in Kings and Chronicles, named in exactly the same manner as "the law of Moses": 2Sam 1:18; 1Ki 8:53; 11:41; 20:11; 22:39; 2Ki 8:23; 14:6; 23:21; 2Chr 23:18; 25:4; 32:32; 33:19; 35:12, 25. This did not just happen in the Old Testament, but also the Apocrypha and Pseudepigrapha. Cf. 1 Es. 3:9; Tob. 1:6; Tbs. 1:6; 1 Ma. 16:24; APS 14:9; T. Levi 5:4; T. Judah 20:3; T. Zebul. 3:4; TMO 1:1; LIV 16:3; ELD 1:1; AEJ 2. To object, "Ah! But these latter texts are not in our canon, but only the Apocrypha and Pseudepigrapha!" is to argue in a circle. The terms are used widely, both inside and outside our Old Testament canon, to refer to quite a number of books outside our current canon. To claim that they mean "Scripture" in some cases, but not in others (because their reference is not to canonical books) is obviously special pleading.

[49] The desperate attempt to salvage the argument against Jude's Enoch quotation is that Hebrews only directly quotes Old Testament texts that are called "Scripture" by other books in the canon. In other words, we use the finished canon to justify our argument for one lone book now in the canon. It also ignores the fairly long list of allusions and similarity of language in Hebrews to other ancient works not in the Old Testament.

Philippians	Titus	**1,2,3John**
Colossians	Philemon	Revelation
1-2Thessalonians		

Would this mean that they don't consider the Old Testament books as *inspired*?

c. At the same time, **all** New Testament books have allusions and/ or comparisons in wording to the *Apocrypha and Pseudepigrapha*, except three: Philemon and 2-3John.

d. These 2 Old Testament books are **never quoted** in any New Testament book: Ruth and Esther. And Esther was not found in the Dead Sea Scrolls. What's more, the book of Esther was not found in the Dead Sea Scrolls. Since they were neither quoted or called *Scripture* by any New Testament book, would this not necessarily mean, according Kruger's approach to Jude, that New Testament writers did not consider these books as inspired or part of the so-called canon?

The result is that calling on the word *graphē* to provide some kind of proof that something was or was not considered inspired is only proof that the methodology has not been thought through.

3. Most Interesting of all: Given Kruger's insistence about what New Testament writers quote and don't quote as Scripture, what should be *shocking* to us as readers is that New Testament authors *don't ever quote from other New Testament documents!* Kruger says (a) these were canonical by the time their ink dried; (b) New Testament authors understood these as being *Scripture*; and (c) these authors were *expecting* a canon to emerge—even though no New Testament document makes any of these claims.

Ok, then, why don't they quote each other? **Luke** overtly refers to "many" gospels, but (using Kruger's wording) does not call them *Scripture*. Luke is possibly even critical of them; and the book of **Acts** (which offers a history of sorts of the earliest church) makes no reference to any kind of "emerging New Testament canon," nor even to any book in that canon," nor even to Paul's letters. Adopting Kruger's logic against the Apocrypha, how can we avoid asking, "Does this mean that New Testament authors did not regard the other New Testament documents as inspired?"

Two texts are usually put forward as proof they did. **2Pt 3:16**, and it is not a *quotation* (I dealt with this text in chapter 2). And **1Tim 5:18**, and it is not a quote of Luke's Gospel, but of a popular proverb, possibly from the oral tradition of Jesus.[50]

Even if we allowed those two examples, what *we* would expect is a robust interplay (a *running conversation*) between New Testament authors (one quoting another), just like we find between Old Testament texts, and also between New Testament authors and Old Testament texts. Based on the sheer numbers of Old Testament texts quoted, it appears (again, using Kruger's logic) that New Testament writers had a far stronger sense of authority from the old sacred scrolls than from the newer Christian texts. In fact, there is far more conversation taking place between New Testament authors and apocryphal and pseudepigraphical texts, than between New Testament texts. The gospels might be described as having a kind of conversation among themselves, but (thinking of Kruger's rules) they never call each other *graphē*. Using that as a standard, Jude regarded 1Enoch more highly than Luke regarded Mark or than John regarded the Synoptics. Does this mean New Testament writers only saw each other's texts as *useful*? Or does it mean this is the wrong kind of issue to impose on New Testament texts? The latter, I think.

Concern #6: Early Christians

Kruger uses the phrase "early Christians" (13 times) in his speech—including "the early Christian movement." He uses the phrase in a "monolithic" manner to mean all Christians who lived in the 1st through the 4th centuries. In the process, he doesn't give

---

[50] See *Collier 2024*, 81; and Fee 1995, 129. (Besides, this approach *demands* an early date for Luke, an assumption most scholars do not accept.)

even a tip of the hat to important sociological and theological up-heavals, nuances, and shifts during that time. (Not even in the 1st century alone.) Nor does he mention how Christians might have evolved or changed or grown in theological awareness, perspective, or expectation. Nor how that might affect attitudes toward the various Christian documents they apparently had began collecting, sometime in the latter half of the 1st century.

There *at least* should be a consideration of the existential crisis among early Christians relating directly to apocalyptic expectations, since many expected Jesus to return "soon," in their lifetime. Even though many 21st century Christians tend to discount this, it is fairly clear that the words of Jesus in Matthew and Luke, and statements in the letters of Paul, Peter, and Revelation can still, to this day, be easily and naturally read as reflecting a widespread expectation of an imminent return of Jesus. (For example, *Marana tha*!) But when Jesus did not come back as expected, this caused a problem.

Let me state this in other words: **Christians did not expect to be a long-lasting community on the earth; Jesus was coming back to get them!** What is arguably Paul's very first letter, 1Thessalonians, is quite clear that at least some first generation Christians were alarmed that some were dying before Jesus' return. When he did not return—especially after 70 CE—the writing down of oral traditions (in various gospels) and the collecting of letters by Paul and others became even more of an urgent matter. One biblical scholar in the mid 20th century quipped something like this:

> The earliest Christians expected Jesus to return;
> what they got, instead, was a growing collection of books.

This is clearly overstated, and it feels stark and harsh. But it carries *at least* a grain of historical and traceable truth. Such realities must be considered in any retelling of "how we got the Bible." I'm not saying this is the only consideration. But it must be an important part of the discussion. Why did questions about "Which documents are ours?"—both among Jews and

Christians—begin showing up in the early second century? Especially since it is so difficult to trace the issue prior to that time.

Such things get entirely left out by Kruger. Instead, he paints "early Christians" with a static, uniform brush. They are described merely as "early Christians," or "the Christian movement," and what is said of later Christians in the 2nd, and 3rd, and even 4th centuries, is used to describe how the earliest Christians felt and acted. (We clearly wouldn't do this with early American history!)

Again, Kruger offers anachronistic representations, and he uses flawed methodology. He also makes no reference to the importance of the shifts from Jewish to Gentile (that is, Greek speaking) Christians; or to the importance of apocalyptic expectations; or to the destruction of Jerusalem in 70 CE, or to the Bar Kochba revolt in 132 CE, or to any other sociological pressure that might have been existing, or waxing and waning, in the early life of the Christian communities. Clearly, Kruger was only giving a speech here; he was not writing a book. But that's not the point. The problem is that his speech presents *a monolithic view of early Christians.* And that is not an accurate representation.

Concern #7: Expecting a New-Covenant Canon

Kruger argues that 1st century Christians *expected* a New Testament canon to be written, and, in fact, that they were looking for written documents from the very start. That's because the nature of *covenant* (a central and key term for Kruger) not only implied but required it. This is as close as he comes to addressing why the New Testament documents never use the term *canon,* and why they never make a claim about the development of a canon. Here, he labors (unsuccessfully) to uncover[51] just how *canon* is inherent within covenant texts.. So he asks:

---

[51] Or, perhaps, *tease* or *pry* this out of texts.

Would Christians have expected a new written collection of books in that New Testament time period? I think they would, given their understanding of what a covenant is.

I think Christianity was the exact, perfect, theological soil, if you will, out of which a new canon would sprout. Yes, they already had an Old Testament canon. But all the pieces were in place that you would expect a New Testament canon to emerge, and emerge very early and very naturally and very organically.[52]

He then maps out his approach:

1. Since they had an old-covenant canon, they were now expecting a new-covenant canon;

2. This canon was planned by God;

3. This canon was needed and it was required by the covenant; and

4. Early Christians believed this canon was currently in the process of coming into existence.

There are some "clear problems" with Kruger's logic.

1. He assumes (and continually asserts) that early Christians already had a well defined Old Testament canon of books—as if that is a well-established fact or a matter of common sense. If he were talking about collections and scrolls that were considered authoritative on one level or another, that would be one thing; but he goes beyond that.

2. He uses these phrases—"Emerged very early," and "very naturally," and "very organically"—as though they are

---

[52] Kruger 2023, starting at 11:34.

the same thing as an *expectation* of the development of a canon.

3. He never addresses why New Testament documents do not quote other New Testament documents. (I've already discussed this as being a problem.)

4. He again directly refers to *a particular set of books*, not simply to a concept of *authority*, when he says this phrase: "the exact, perfect, theological soil, if you will, out of which *a new canon* would sprout." He means by this a specific set of authoritative, inspired documents.

Concern #8: Covenant Written on the Heart?

Some of the things Kruger writes about covenant and related issues are quite reasonable. Whether any of it has anything to do with "a canon of written texts" is another question. So what do we say about a covenant that is to be "written on the heart"? For in this discussion, Jer 31:31-33 surely comes to mind:

> "Behold, the days are coming," says the LORD, "when I will make a new covenant with the house of Israel and the house of Judah, [32] not like the covenant which I made with their fathers when I took them by the hand to bring them out of the land of Egypt, my covenant which they broke, though I was their husband, says the LORD. [33] But this is the covenant which I will make with the house of Israel after those days, says the LORD: **I will put my law within them, and I will write it upon their hearts**; and I will be their God, and they shall be my people."

Kruger does not address this in this speech, but he does address this in his book *The Question of Canon* pp. 110-11. There he says that this text is meant to address *intent* of writing, not to an intent *to keep things oral*. In his treatment, he is fighting against those who (he says) now claim that God never intended a written canon, only oral teaching.

I agree that we should be careful not to overread Jeremiah, as though Jeremiah were forbidding anyone to write anything down. But it might speak to where New Testament writers (esp. Heb 8:8-9:28) were focused when quoting it. It wasn't on a new set of books. When Paul calls himself a "minister of a new covenant" in 2Cor 3:6,

> . . . who has made us competent to be **ministers of a new covenant**, not in a written code but in the Spirit; for the written code kills, but the Spirit gives life,

he gives no indication that he is fighting against any written document simply *because* it is written. Rather, he's fighting a Jew-Gentile battle on the Gentile frontier of his Christian mission, based on his own experience every Sabbath, where readers of holy texts (in his view) can become so buried in those texts, and the traditions that engulf them, that they can no longer breathe their life-giving message. (We all have experienced this in our own Christian gatherings.) If Paul were throwing out sacred texts, he would not have wasted his time conversing midrashically with Exodus 34 throughout this chapter—a veil over their eyes, indeed! That said, a new set of books is not on Paul's mind.

Kruger labors intensely to keep this "new covenant written on the heart" idea away from his notion that Christians expected a new canon of documents. As noted earlier, the problem for Kruger's case about "a needed new canon" is that no such claim is ever made for such a thing. It is one thing to say that Paul expected his readers to follow his spirit-led guidance and instructions; it's another thing entirely to say that Paul thought he was writing an inspired new book for the expected new canon. That Christian readers *welcomed* new writings is clear. But what this indicates (instead of an expectation of a new canon) is that *they were open to such guidance and had no concept that they were not allowed to accept new writings as authoritative, beneficial, and helpful*. Whether they initially put all of this on the same level as the Torah is a different question altogether. In fact, it is surely absurd to think that he would have written anything like this,

> "My writings
> —only the ones God intends for the new canon—
> are, like the Torah: holy, and just, and good!"

If there is any place in New Testament documents that could have easily talked about "the coming new canon," it would have been in 2Corinthians 3. How is such a new canon going to be "written on the heart?" Would that not be an obvious, or even necessary question? (Acts 15 is another such text; and Heb 8-9 another.) No New Testament text talks about an expected new canon because that was not an issue in New Testament texts or for Christians in the 1st century, as far as can be determined.

Hence, there is no indication from our biblical or related texts that such a thing as a God-ordained, closed canon of books was either promised or expected.

In the next chapter—chapter 4—I'll look at concerns 9 and 10: misleading statements by Kruger, and the tone of his public speech.

–4–

Misleading Statements & Tone

This chapter will focus on concerns 9 and 10.

Concern #9: Misleading Statements

Kruger makes several statements that are misleading.

a. The so-called, "planned," biblical canon

It's one thing for Kruger to say, "it makes sense," that new documents might or would appear, and that, over time, they might become important. But it's another to use such evidence as *proof* that a specific canon was planned by God from the start. This is an assumption that no biblical text claims, and cannot be proved.

b. The oversimplified "core of documents"

It is understandable that Kruger wishes to dispel any notion of a "free-for-all attitude" in the second century, as if everybody regarded as *authoritative* whatever books they pleased. And it's useful to note that Christians "regarded highly" a particular core of documents from the 1st century. For example, Kruger says,

> The reality is Christians didn't widely disagree about the books. In fact what's interesting is that they were settled on a core collection of books shockingly early.

39

But it is not helpful to cast this in terms of a focused "canon consciousness" in the early 2nd century or to present it in such an oversimplified manner.

1. When Kruger says "settled," he leaves an impression that Christians in the early 2nd century were collectively of pretty much a single mind in trying to decide on which books were "in" and which were "out." Actually, it's too early for that.

2. When Kruger uses the phrase "early Christians" in this part of his speech (he says it 3 times starting at the 23:36 marker of his video speech), this can only refer to Christians in the 2nd century and later, not to those in the 1st century.

3. However, when Kruger says the phrase "shockingly early," this is misleading because just how early is highly debatable. Some of this rests on a particular date given to the Muratorian fragment (was it 2nd or 4th century?), as well as other technical issues.

4. The fact that he admits that there is any kind of core *with fuzzy edges* means, in fact, there was no finally agreed-upon, closed list of books. This can surely be seen as an emerging, canon-consciousness-in-the-making, in the 2nd through the 4th centuries—a consciousness that increased as time went along. But it's not as if Christian thinkers saw themselves on some kind of celestial, centuries-long, mission or trajectory to finally recognize the one, true, divinely intended canon that God had established before creation.

There was clearly a growing interest in questions that would eventually lead to a standardized list of books by the end of the 4th century. But this grew, primarily, as a response to the incessant rise of teachings deemed false. As noted earlier, in chapter one, this was the very language used by Athanasius of Alexandria in 367 CE; namely, for the purpose of combating false teaching—

to set forth in order the books that are canonized, transmitted, and believed to be divine.

This is not the language of a supposed, divine canon, promised from before the foundation of the world. It is rather of particular books believed to be inspired, now set forth as *canonized* (i.e., recognized as having authority) by the churches.

So, just because we can, in *retrospect*, see some kind of historical trajectory lasting four centuries, does not mean anyone, in *prospect*, had any awareness or belief they were embarking on a four-century-long assigned mission of recognizing an already existing canon, which was yet to be discovered.

So then, from very early on, there were some significant differences in various localities over the use of books like the Shepherd of Hermas, the Didache, or 1st Clement, the Letter of Barnabas, the Apocalypse of Peter, Hebrews, James, 2Peter, 2-3John, Jude, and Revelation. Those differences are hardly minor.

Furthermore, this has implications about how Christians were viewing the collections of writings during the latter half of the 1st century. Namely, if there had been any sense that they had an assigned mission from God to be about the business of recognizing the new canon God has already given to them, then what happened to that "sense"? Does anyone claim such a mission? Did it disappear or go underground by the early 2nd century?

c. *The Council of Trent*

In the Q&A session, Kruger states about the Apocrypha,

> Well, it was adopted formally in what's called the Council of Trent in the 16th century as sort of a counter-Reformation move. That's the first time the church officially received those books—that is, the Roman Catholic Church.

His key phrase, here, is, "adopted formally." But this is both misleading, and a bit ironic. Here's why.

1. Kruger's statement is misleading because one could easily think he was saying that the Apocrypha was not part of the Roman Catholic canon till it was added at the Council of Trent—which, of course, is not correct. (I'm not suggesting that Kruger doesn't know what the Council of Trent was or did—of course he does—only that his quick statement was insufficient and open to misinterpretation.) It is more accurate to say that Trent reaffirmed that the Apocrypha had been a central issue in the canon discussion in the Roman Catholic Church since the 4th century.

Three church councils are significant for this question: the Council of Rome (382 CE), the Council of Florence (1431–1449 CE) and the Council of Trent (1545–1563 CE.

The followers of Jerome (who rejected the Apocrypha) and Augustine (who accepted it) had debated their positions for a thousand years, and this debate was respected by the Council of Trent, which did not attempt to resolve it.[53] According to O'Malley, interpreters took the council Trent to have officially sanctioned the Apocrypha as fully canonical. However, what Trent did, in fact, was to reaffirm, officially, that the Apocrypha had been part of the canon question since the 4th century. This included the longstanding internal debate over the Apocrypha, going on since the time of Jerome and Augustine. Yes, Trent was a counter-Reformation move, because Luther in particular had challenged and demoted the Apocrypha, along with seven New Testament books; namely, Hebrews, James, 2Peter, 2-3John, Jude, and Revelation—the books that had the most difficult time being included during the first four centuries. Trent, in effect, stepped in to say, "Not so fast! This is the way it's been for the biblical canon throughout the whole history of the church. And this is the way it's going to stay."

2. Kruger's statement is ironic because he rejects the notion that the church *chose* any book for the canon—unless we are talking

---

[53] The study of O'Malley 2013 is especially important understanding Trent.

about the Apocrypha. In that case, "the Catholic church 'formally adopted' the Apocrypha," but only at the Council of Trent.

d. Free-for-all vs fluidity

Kruger caricatures and then downplays the amount of fluidity that existed in the first three centuries.

> I hear this all the time both in the academy, and just even in the church. Sadly this idea that no one could agree on books, everyone had their own canon, no one could get along, everyone had their own little collection of books, some are reading that book and some are reading this book—it's a big mess everybody's got their own little collections they're using! It's sort of this literary free-for-all!

It may be that some individuals have such an impression (thank you Dan Brown!), but I know of no canon scholar who would say such a thing as this. Kruger is right that a "free-for-all" would be a mis-impression.

However, New Testament documents *do* reflect a situation in the 1st century in which Christians were reading from a large pool of Hebrew and Greek sacred literature that had somewhat fluid edges. Lee Martin McDonald is certainly right to compare Josephus's so-called "22 book canon" with the library at Qumran and then conclude that, "there was no universally accepted, closed biblical canon in the first century CE" [54]

Furthermore, there is no indication that 1st century Christians displayed *any* interest or need in defining "edges." Nor was there any terminology at this time for talking about canonical or non-canonical documents. As stated, this does *not* imply a "free-for-all"; but it *does* indicate that there was no traceable pursuit of a

---

[54] McDonald 2007, 150-160, especially 156. See also McDonald 2020, 81f, esp. about Josephus.

concern over which books were "in" or "out." Five important facts help to illustrate this point:

1. The fact that there were some significant collections of books (like the centrality of the Torah and the importance of the Prophets) and that these were being recognized above others does not imply that anyone was interested in excluding or hemming books in.

2. The fact that Christians had no trouble adding new writings to the list of previous ones shows that they had no concept of a "closed" group of sacred texts.

3. The fact that most New Testament writers quote from Greek scrolls and not Hebrew shows that, for them, the language of the texts was not an issue.

4. The fact that there are demonstrable allusions to Hellenistic writings as inspired writings indicates at least some level of openness and fluidity.

5. Finally, the codex (like our current-day "books," with pages written on both sides, and with a spine of some kind), was not at all common until well after the 1st century. The earliest evidence for the existence of the codex is the 1st century CE. It began replacing scrolls during the 2nd to the 4th centuries. [55] The codex was an important factor in the developing of a canon since, now, it was possible to have various documents contained in a single book. This fact alone made the idea of "what belongs *in* our Bible" a non-asked question. There was no such thing as a "Bible."

---

[55] See Roberts 1983, 38ff. See also Watson 2019, 5, "The rise of Christianity to its fourth century cultural dominance is coextensive with the rise of the codex." And also 17, "'The Bible' as we know it is the result not just of authorial activity, divinely inspired or otherwise, but also of evolving techniques of book production."

Concern #10: Tone

I have a final and general comment about the tone of the speech. Despite all of my critical comments to this point, Kruger obviously and commendably is passionate about this topic. He gave a generally positive and energetic public lecture to a friendly lay audience. It was upbeat and more relaxed than an academic paper. For many who love the Bible, Kruger's message about canon will be attractive, compelling, and reassuring. His approach will engender trust, and his message is bound to win many grateful followers (mainly among conservative Christians). For them, his approach will breathe new life into the waning traditional arguments about the biblical canon.

However, as I have indicated through these chapters, his approach leaves me, quite simply, out of breath. As a lifelong, serious student of the Bible myself, I offer my critique openly and respectfully, despite the accolades for Kruger's position from scholars, preachers, and readers alike. I do not have the same responses. In his speech, it's probably natural that he "played to his audience" now and then, but this occasionally devolved into a dismissive or condescending tone, especially against those who might not share some of his theological presuppositions.

In these chapters, I have tried to show why I find his approach and arguments deeply flawed, and why I consider them harmful, in the long run, to how the church understands and presents the Bible to itself and to the world. In a nutshell, it sets believers up for a hard fall when they realize the circular weakness of the case.

With that statement, I've now completed my list of 10 concerns about Kruger's one hour public address. As a kind of summary, in the next chapter—chapter 5—I'll offer a point-by-point reply to each of Kruger's 7 listed "misconceptions." This will bring a certain amount of repetition, but I hope it will function as a succinct summary of my critique of his approach.

—5—

Responses to the "7 Misconceptions"

Review/Summary

In the previous four chapters, I've discussed my top 10 concerns about Michael Kruger's public address.

a. I *noted and discussed* 3 major preconceptions that underlie his pronouncements; *challenged* his concept and application of the word *canon*; and *underscored* problems with his notion of (what I called) the "supernatural selection" of canonical books, as well as his insistence that all canonical books are self-authorizing *as canon*.

b. I *pointed* to his inappropriate and problematic interchangeable use of the words *canon, authority,* and collections of books; *highlighted* how he depicts early Christians as if they were a more or less uniform group; and *confronted* his insistence that the writers of the New Testament documents *expected* a New Testament canon.

c. I *critiqued* how he essentially side-steps the biblical statement "the covenant written on the heart"; and I *reviewed* some of his overstatements and misleading comments in a public presentation that aimed to be correctional, but which sometimes feels condescending.

d.   Finally, I evaluated *specific* texts; and I **contested** several key, long-standing interpretations of some specific New Testament texts, including vocabulary.

So, now, in this chapter, I'll give a direct, short response to each one of what he calls, "the 7 misconceptions about canon."

Responses to the "7 Misconceptions"

Misconception #1:

Kruger says, many people have the misconception that, *early Christians who had heard about Jesus, and heard the message of the gospel, did not even think there would be a new canon!*

My reply: In fact, there is no evidence that 1st century Jews and Christians thought in terms of canon. Authority? Yes! Canon? No! (And, no, these are not the same.) They certainly read from books they considered authoritative and/or sacred. And those varied somewhat in language, value, and number. When Kruger insists that canon means authority, and not a list of books, it turns out that that is not what actually happens in practice. When the word *canon* is used, there invariably comes a point that the word begins to bleed with double meanings and imported baggage. Also, "a new set of books" never comes up in any biblical text; no biblical text gives any indication there would ever be such a set of books. The result is that *canon* is a later theological construct, anachronistically read onto biblical texts.

Misconception #2:

Kruger says, many people have the misconception that, *the authors of the New Testament did not think they were writing scripture!*

My reply: In fact, the only New Testament document that claims to be an inspired document is the book of Revelation, one of the books Luther called into question, and which "was not fully accepted into the Greek Orthodox canon until the seventeenth century, and it has never formed a part of the Orthodox liturgy."[56] Paul's claims of authority in texts like 1Cor 7:40 and 9:8; or in 2Cor 10:8 or 13:10. These are not claims by Paul about the inspiration of his writings, or that the letter is now part of an emerging canon. He is certainly, and very clearly, making a claim about the authority given him by God for the specific content of his gospel message. It is only by mashing the terms *authority*, *canon*, and *inspiration* together, and pretending that they all mean or imply the same thing, that Kruger can anachronistically call upon such texts as proof of canon.

Misconception #3:

Kruger says, many people have the misconception that, *early Christians disagreed widely over which books belonged in the New Testament!*

My reply: As best we can tell, the concerns about whether books were in or out began ramping up around Marcion's time and after (about 130 CE or so), especially in the face of various perceived threats to the faith. Whether there was a core commonly used or not about this time, there was also an array of other documents being used; so, there was no settled, unified, group of documents for 200 to 400 more years. Even then, the apocrypha was never completely accepted by all—the heirs of Jerome standing against those documents as secondary. Of course, in 16th century reformation, there was upheaval again over this question.

---

[56] Gallagher/Mead 2017, 279, who speaks also about cracks in the Western tradition.

Misconception #4:

Kruger says, many people have the misconception that, *there was no canon until the 4th or 5th century!*

My reply: It is demonstrable that there was no settled canon till then or after, and even then, there were objections by Jerome and followers over the apocrypha. Much later, martin Luther stirred up protestants for a century when he re-challenged the apocrypha for the Old Testament, and Hebrews, James, 2Peter, 2-3John, Jude, and Revelation for the New Testament—all books that had faced serious contests when being accepted into the canon in the first place.

Misconception #5:

Kruger says, many people have the misconception that, *apocryphal books are just as valid as the New Testament books!*

My reply: If canon is viewed as the one true canon created by God for the church (as Kruger uses it), then the term *valid* means one thing; if canon is understood as the best efforts of the church to follow God, *valid* might be *more or less valid* for various readers or church traditions. It is a fact that apocryphal books are still included in some Christian canons. In some cases, they are deemed of secondary value, so not as *valid*. The Protestant canon that exists today excludes them, even though, originally, they were included in a secondary location. There is a sense in which a firm canon is more of a theological and political theory than a reality, because nearly all Christians (and nearly all churches) have a functional canon within the canon, which means they find some books more valuable than others.

Misconception #6:

Kruger says, many people have the misconception that, *apocryphal books were as popular as New Testament books!*

My reply: Some might have been as popular as some New Testament books in some places for a while: e.g., 2Peter and Revelation. Eventually, for most of them, that changed. Partly because they were excluded or demoted, or because they might have been brought into wide use at a later time (like 2Peter). How one judges the popularity of books might depend on the time and local usage.

Misconception #7:

Kruger says, many people have the misconception that, *the New Testament books were picked by the church!*

My reply: As a matter of fact, *of course* they were picked by the church! That's why we find a variety of canons among Christians worldwide. Not all Christians everywhere exactly agree on the matter. But here's a question: who passed the law that there could be only one acceptable canon in the world? Since there is no *claim* in biblical texts that God promised a single, once-for-all canon, is it just *possible* that God can be involved in all of the current competing canonical traditions?

There Can Be Only One

Summarizing to this point: In chapters 1 through 4, I offered 10 major concerns about Kruger's argument. In the present chapter, I succinctly replied to each of his 7 so-called, misconceptions. By now, it is clear that, in my view, Kruger's case is faulty from the ground up.

I'm not alone in my critique. As I noted in chapter 2, above, Michael Bird and N. T. Wright, in their 2019 book, *The New Testament in Its World* were quite critical of this kind of approach.

> There are many who, taught to believe the Bible, treat the New Testament canon as a self-evident and self-authorizing collection. For them, it would only be a slight caricature to say that the Church Fathers, like early versions of

Indiana Jones, went searching for scriptures, finding hidden scrolls in ancient catacombs or sneaking into imperial palaces to steal confiscated copies of the gospels. Then, equipped with some kind of magic device for telling which documents were inspired, they added their freshly discovered texts to their collection of what became holy scriptures. [57]

But they don't stop here. They continue with the following positive suggestion:

The New Testament canon, however, was neither artificially invented by authorities nor discovered by Bible-questing adventurers. The church did not create the word of God. Rather, the church itself is a *creatura verbum dei*, "a creature of the word of God." Jesus himself, the incarnate word, and the apostolic word of the gospel, are what call, gather, encourage, admonish, and sustain the church. However, the church, with all its discussions, debates, and decisions, was the instrument by which the inspired word of apostolic testimony was put into its canonical location, to be seen as an authoritative collection of sacred texts. In other words, canonization, is a shorthand way of referring to God's sanctifying work in the ecclesiastical processes that led to the compilation and promulgation of the New Testament canon.

This is a much different path than Kruger offers: namely, God working within and through the church's canon efforts not so the church can somehow, *discover*, all the correct, predetermined canon books, as if they are easter eggs scattered around by God; but rather, as God's working through the church.

But what does their phrase actually mean, "God's sanctifying work in the ecclesiastical processes"? It certainly sounds holy. Their very next paragraph (which I'll quote momentarily) ap-

---

[57] Bird & Wright, 2019, 867. They do not specifically mention Kruger.

pears to assume two things: (1) that God's ultimate goal for his "sanctifying work in the ecclesiastical processes" is to end up with only one true canon; and (2) that human beings have just not quite got there yet. In this one respect, they appear to agree with Kruger and a host of other approaches, that there is only supposed to be one canon. Note the word *admittedly* as I quote that statement.

> *Admittedly*, there remains to this day a multiplicity of biblical canons. Catholics, Protestants, Greek Orthodox, and Oriental Orthodox Christians have, interestingly, different collections. This, however, affects the Old Testament rather than the New. There is firm consensus about the main constituent parts of the New Testament canon that are shared by all forms of Christianity across the globe. [58]

The word *admittedly*, here, feels somewhat apologetic, almost as if God has a grand, end-goal for canon, and that, unfortunately, people have just not yet fully figured it out. So, if Kruger's approach[59] is, Indiana Jones, it appears that Bird and Wright tap into the Duncan MacLeod approach, of Highlander fame—that TV series in which immortals chop off each other's heads week after week while repeating the phrase, "There can be only one!"

Furthermore, the phrase "firm consensus about the main constituent parts" is vague and betrays some abiding differences in some parts, not only in the New Testament but also the Old. It's like asking someone, "How do you feel?" and getting a response, "For the most part, good!" Apparently, not all is well. So even though there are large agreements over canon, there are still differences. And those continued differences after thousands of years rightly call into question what we mean by canon.

---

[58] Bird & Wright, 2019, 867, my italics.

[59] They do not mention Kruger by name or work.

One has to wonder whether the apparent assumption (that there can or should be only one divinely sanctioned biblical canon) is serving the larger discussion. Does it *naturally grow out* of the available evidence? Or is it a *growth foisted upon* the available evidence, predetermining the outcome? To put this more directly, a couple of questions seem logical and in order at this point:

a. Is it possible that God never planned a one-size-fits-all canon, and that Christian existence, reality, and unity transcend the size and form of a particular canonical shape?

b. Is it possible that God uses the church's Bible, in whatever canonical diversity that exists, to assist in his grand conversation with human kind?

In the next chapter, I'll turn to the difference between canon and sacred texts. In the process, I'll raise an issue about unasked and unanswered questions. I'll then offer four considerations when thinking about canon.

Part II:
Redirecting the
Canon Question

—6—

Redirecting the Canon Question

How can we, as Christians, *"know* that we have the right twenty-seven books in our New Testament?" That's how Kruger begins his 2012 book. [60] This is probably the most often asked question about canon (especially by non-specialists), so he didn't make it up.

But it's the wrong question. It merely assumes there is such a thing as a "right" collection of books intended by God. As often happens in old Perry Mason shows, this assumes a fact not in evidence.

I suggest that nothing short of a full-blown paradigm shift is both already underway and needed for how we understand and apply the concepts of scripture, canon, and inspiration.

In this chapter, I'll attempt to redirect the question from, "Are we sure we have the right 27 books?" to a more appropriate and productive approach. I'll begin by pointing out three macro-problem areas in Kruger's program.

---

[60] Kruger 2012, 15, his italics.

1. Unasked Questions

Here are two fundamental questions that I have been unable to find in Kruger's materials.

> Whose idea was canon to start with?
>
> Does any biblical text even claim that a finalized, "one true inspired canon" was God's idea or intent?

These are, actually, fairly big questions simply to assume. Even so, for many, they are startling or even jolting. Why would anyone ask such questions? Also, they seem to imply a binary choice: either a divine origin or a human origin.

Kruger implicitly tries to shoot down any notion of a human origin in two ways:

He says there was no Dan Brown "smoke-filled room" for selecting New Testament books. To whatever extent he is correct about that specific scenario, that doesn't eliminate church leaders from having a fundamental role, over 8 to 10 generations, during the 2nd and 4th centuries, *selecting* which books were being read in the churches.

But more importantly, he overtly and unapologetically turns to a particular brand of theology to provide what he cannot show from explicit claims in biblical texts. So, in the absence of overt textual claims, he turns to theological innuendo and speculation.

2. Historical Criteria

Specifically, as pointed out in chapter 5, Kruger relies on an easter-egg approach; namely, what God does not say directly about which books belong in the canon, he has left as hints scattered in texts, concepts, and undisclosed places. We (i.e., the church) just have to know how to "discover" which books are already in God's predetermined canon.

However, if God left directions or criteria for how to *discover* this already divinely decided canon, neither Kruger nor anyone else has been able to identify them. Certainly, one can dig around in history to find the various and scattered "criteria" that were actually used by various churches and their leaders to determine if books were

1. widely used
2. thought to be apostolic/prophetic
3. approved by Jesus or the apostles
4. considered to be inspired
5. without heretical teachings
6. in concert with other accepted Scripture books
7. (or other such things)

But even if these criteria are said to be, "God working in the church through the Holy Spirit" to "*recognize* [not select] God's predestined canon," there still remain several problems for Kruger's position:

First and most importantly, even using the above criteria, the worldwide church ended up producing various canons that differed from each other to one degree or another. The *fact* is, to this day, no worldwide, unanimously settled canon has ever existed. A truly *settled* canon has only happened within individual Christian traditions.

Second, there never was a single or clear list of such criteria or church-wide agreement about them. McDonald states this plainly:

> No surviving evidence suggests that all churches used the same criteria in selecting their sacred collections. Likewise, no evidence suggests that each separate criterion weighed equally with others in deliberations about canon. . . . The

most common criteria employed in the canonical process
include apostolicity, orthodoxy, antiquity, and use. [61]

Third, not even the New Testament canon has been regarded as
all that settled. For example, more than *eleven full centuries* (!) after
Athanasius' list of "canonized" New Testament books, Luther apparently did not think of the New Testament as all that settled.
That's why he was able to rise up in protest and question seven
specific books of the New Testament canon, including Hebrews
and Revelation. After a hundred years of debate, he wasn't followed in this, but he *was* followed in excluding the Apocrypha.
I've also mentioned a time or two the somewhat schizophrenic
attitudes about the book of Revelation in the early centuries in the
West (e.g., Eusebius lists it both as accepted and spurious); and
not until the 17th century in the Greek Orthodox church. [62]

Fourth, the fact that, today, the differences in canon worldwide
have *mostly* to do with Old Testament books does not resolve the
"predetermined canon" problem. In fact, not all churches have
identical New Testaments (for example, the Tewahedo churches
of Eritrea and Ethiopia has eight or so additional books in their
New Testament, and a total of 81 in their biblical canon). If a "predetermined canon" by God is to mean anything at all, then it must
apply to the entire canon (Old Testament and New Testament).
And by no stretch of the imagination can it be claimed that the
worldwide church has a single canon. [63]

The bottom line for all of this is that the worldwide church—two
thousand years down the line—still to this day does not know

---

[61] McDonald 2007, 405:

[62] Gallagher/Mead 2017, 100, esp. 104, and 278.

[63] It is one thing to say this theoretically in passing (and it can be easily dismissed or
glossed over), but it is a more gripping point to see the varied lists side by side. See
McDonald 2007, 439-451; and also Gallagher/Mead 2017.

what "God's one and only predetermined canon" is supposed to be![64]

3. Provincial Thinking

Because all of us who identify as Christians *tend* to think from inside our own denominational cocoons, we also *tend* to view our own canon as the benchmark from which to consider the larger questions. [65] Since we all think we already know what the canon is or is supposed to be, there is no kind of widespread realization of the fact that, as a whole, the Christian world has never had a settled canon. This is still shocking—or even scandalous—to many Christians.

But regardless of denominational background, we surely have to ask why, to this day, do we remain at such an unsettled[66] position worldwide? If a specific Old/New Testament single canon was God's idea, and the church was supposed to "discover the books that were already in God's canon," then after two thousand years, either the clues are too hard, or we also have to figure out which Christian tradition is the right group to have figured it out. East? West? Catholic? Protestant? Reformed? Lutheran? Arminian? Mormon?[67] Other?

But do any of us really want to go down that rabbit hole? I (along with many other Christians) grew up with this as a dominant question; namely, "Which is the one, true church?" It's a waste of time and a dead-end road.

---

[64] To whatever degree, large or small, is not the point. The worldwide canon is still varied.

[65] Unfortunately, Kruger's approach suffers from just such a malady.

[66] I do not distinguish between the words *unsettled canon* (in the church) and *closed canon* (by God as soon as written) as Kruger 2012, 280. A canon is closed when the community considers it closed.

[67] Certainly the question could be pressed beyond Christianity, if one is asking what God *intended*.

The unasked question, "Whose idea was canon in the first place?" deserves a better answer than simply to assume that it was *God's* idea and that everybody should merely genuflect.

This is why the questions at the end of the previous chapter call out for reply:

1. Is it possible that God never planned a "one size fits all" canon, and that Christian existence, reality, and unity transcend the size and form of a particular canonical shape?

2. Is it possible that God uses the church's Bible, in whatever canonical diversity that exists, to assist in his grand conversation with humankind?

These questions will form the basis of the next chapter which will discuss four fundamental considerations that need to be seriously addressed about canon.

— 7 —

Fundamentals for Canon

To address the two questions at the end of the previous chapter, I'll now launch a discussion of four fundamental considerations for rethinking canon. These are fundamental issues for a new paradigm when thinking about canon.

1. Scripture & Canon

First and foremost, we need to take seriously the difference between the words *scripture* and *canon*. As I have indicated in previous chapters, these words have only come to be blurred and muddled into each other since the late 18th century, to the point that they are now virtually interchangeable. (And by this I mean, in every case, that one implies the other.) But this is a critical mistake when referring to the Bible. They do not mean the same thing.

    a. The word *scripture* is more correctly translated from the Greek word *graphē* in the New Testament as *texts, scrolls, or books*. And contextually, these are generally considered to be inspired of God. This word carries no hint or implication of an existing or "soon to be coming" specific list or canon of books.[68]

---

[68] See a similar paragraph in McDonald 2007, 54. He does not go far enough in distinguishing the words *scripture* and *canon*. As I've indicated, based on the thorough

63

    b. The word *kanōn* in the New Testament never refers to books, and it is certainly not used for a promised list of books as some kind of predetermined, authoritative entity. Any use of the term *canon* for what is going on within biblical documents turns out to be mere anachronism.

Now, there is no question that in many current-day discussions, these words are *intentionally* used interchangeably. In approaches like Kruger's, this interchangeability is necessary for the theology he proposes! However, this is both anachronistic and fundamentally wrong-headed.

The result is that both words (scripture and canon) are being misused in discussions today to bolster theological positions about the Bible that cannot be supported from biblical texts themselves.

I brought this out specifically in chapter 2 where I mention that the word *graphē* occurs about 50 times in the New Testament for a writing, or a whole book, or an undefined collection of writings.[69] To go further, now: in contrast, the word *kanōn* never refers to books even once in biblical and related literature.[70] Ironically, the word comes close to being used in an "anti-book"[71] manner in Gal 6:11-16, where Paul steps out from behind the

-----

study in Collier 2024, the word *scripture* is now so loaded with theological baggage that it should be dropped entirely as a translation of the Greek word *graphē*.

  [69] Based on the indepth word study in Collier 2018/2024.

  [70] The point is not that the word never occurs in biblical and related literature; it is rather that it does not refer to any kind of "list of books," nor is it ever used to show the *authority* of books. The word is used mainly for a rule or standard one's own life is to follow, or a particular teaching as a "rule of faith." In the **Old Testament** 1 time: Mic 7:4. In the **New Testament** 4 times: 2Cor 10:13, 15, 16; Gal 6:1. In **Apocrypha** 2 times: Jdt. 13:6; 4 Ma. 7:21. In **Philo** 27 times: Leg. 3:233; Sacr. 1:59; Det. 1:125; Post. 1:28, 104; Gig. 1:49; Agr. 1:130; Ebr. 1:185; Conf. 1:2; Her. 1:154, 160, 173; Fug. 1:152; Somn. 1:73; Ios. 1:145; Mos. 1:76; Decal. 1:14, 140; Spec. 1:287; 3:137, 164; 4:115; Virt. 1:70, 219; Prob. 1:83; Aet. 1:108, 116. In **Josephus** only 2 times: Ant. 10:49; Apion 2:174. In the **Pseudepigrapha** 3 times: T. Naph. 2:3; Aris. 1:2; 4 Ma. 7:21.

  [71] This is a tongue-in-cheek overstatement. Paul is certainly not "anti-book," here. However, it is used in the very context of obedience to the Torah, where the word *kanōn* is referring, not to the Torah, but to the concept of the New Creation.

curtain to "write with his own hand," against those Christian teachers who make a big show of following the Torah, and who require circumcision so as to avoid being persecuted. But Paul objects:

> [15] For neither circumcision is anything, nor uncircumcision; instead, "A new creation!" [16] So, as many as adhere strictly to this *rule* [i.e., "to this *kanōn*"], may peace be upon them, and mercy—even upon the Israel of God! (Gal 6:15-16)

The *canon* in this text is not the Torah, or indeed any book or collection of books. The word is used, rather, in *contrast to* the hypocritical way Torah is being "obeyed." For the Apostle Paul, the *canon* is the life-giving reality of the New Creation—the *standard*, the *rule*.

This use of the word *kanōn* in Greek literature is precisely what was pointed out in 1968 by Rudolf Pfeiffer (whom I quoted at length in chapter 1):

> one has the impression that most people who use it [the word *kanōn*] believe that this usage is of Greek origin. But *kanōn* was never used in this sense, nor would this have been possible. From its frequent use in ethics *kanōn* always retained the meaning of rule or model.

Neither Paul or any other biblical writer shows any concern with an emerging, closed collection of books, or with a supposed promise of such.

When we use *scripture* to mean or imply *canon*, we ascribe to that word a meaning that it never had.

But more than that, something else happens: when we think the word scripture implies canon, *we change our own focus from "holy texts" to "holy canon."* It's from this point on that we subtly, but unequivocally, begin speaking the language of "inspired canon." And from there, we start asking, "Which canon is the *right* canon?

Someone will object: "You say holy *texts*," but I say "holy *canon*" — it's all the same thing!"

No, it is not.

This is reminiscent of an entire religious movement whose commendable motto in the 19th century was, "We are Christians only!" However, by the mid 20th century that had become "We are the only Christians!" This is a subtle shift with huge ramifications. The same is true with canon. It makes a difference whether we speak of "holy texts" or "holy canon."

2. God's Idea

Second, we need to come face to face with the cold, hard fact that no biblical text makes any claim that God had planned or ordained a specific closed canon of holy texts. It is not heretical to recognize this *fact* about biblical texts, and it is not spiritual or faithful to force our own theological speculations and theories back into biblical texts to make them say what they don't. If biblical texts don't claim it, we should not be saying they do.

3. The Church in Conversation with God

Third, we need to give more attention to how God works through the church in its concern over holy texts, and how the church is in conversation with God through those texts. Since there is no biblical warrant that a "one, true, final, canon of holy texts" was God's idea, the question then becomes, "How has God worked through the various biblical collections of holy texts as one way of accomplishing his will in the world?" This concern would take into account and show respect for — and perhaps even honor and celebrate — the historical reality throughout Christian history of the emergence of multiple biblical collections of holy texts, where the specific lists of holy texts don't exactly agree. (Frankly, the concern over "which Christian canon is the one, true, required, right biblical canon," is just another brand of the question, "Which is the one and only true church?")

What we *don't* need is the imposition of a supposed, specific, pre-destined canon based on contrived arguments. All this does is set up Christians young and old for a Humpty Dumpty-type fall when they come to realize the arguments are overstatements and theories that will not stand up to a close textual and historical scrutiny. At such times, shattered faith can become impossible to piece together again.

What we *do* need is broad-based specific attention to how God works in the world through the worldwide church and through the multiform canons it has produced.

a. Such attention would be consistent with the explicit claims of biblical texts, like 2Tim 3:14ff or 2Pt 1:20f and others (as these were discussed at length above in chapters 1-5), without overreading those claims through anachronism and other wishful theological thinking. Biblical texts should be attended to according to their own contexts and in terms of what they actually claim, rather than what we might wish them to claim.

b. Such attention would seriously focus on how our variety of biblical canons *in fact* arose, not only in the fight against heresies, but also in widely varied live church settings where different issues were being addressed, in different languages and across ethnic and national lines. (There should be no assumption that the church everywhere dealt with a flat set of issues in a fixed or programmatic manner.) It would also evaluate how the church worldwide "binds and looses" in different ways on matters relating to canonical concerns, and how that might be watching God at work through various church traditions.

c. Such attention would consider the fact that there is no claim of God planning a "one size fits all" canon, and that Christian existence might actually transcend the size and form of a particular canonical shape.

d. Such attention would consider whether the biblical canons from the four corners of the earth function, perhaps, like the four gospels that tell the story of Jesus in different ways, by different authors, to different people, at different times, and for different reasons. It would at least *think* about such a comparison.

e. Perhaps such attention would even *celebrate* the variety of canon lists of holy texts from around the earth as a witness to the God who cannot be contained in any temple, and who cannot be confined within any one form of a conventionally fashioned single book. Perhaps it would revel in the fact that God uses "the Bible"—that multi-form "book" in all its canonical diversity—to carry on a grand conversation with all of humankind.

f. Such attention would be careful when evaluating whether God could *not*, or could *only*, work through particular collections of documents.

g. And of course, such attention would necessarily consider questions about non-traditional canons (like the Mormon canon or the Eritrean and Ethiopian Tewahedo canon), and even ancient historical efforts (like the so-called Marcionite canon).

Now, when pointing to such things, I was asked recently: "Are you saying that canonical efforts are a waste of time? That we should abandon them? That they are *merely* human efforts?" No, no, and no. That's not what I said at all. Efforts to evaluate holy texts are natural and valuable. Canons of all kinds can be quite valuable. And we should focus on how God is active in canonical processes, just as he has always been active in the world, and now through the church for the world's sake.

4. Megaphone or Conversation Table

Fourth, we need to understand canon less like God's megaphone, and more like a conversation table for diverse biblical authors and their texts.

(a) When seeing canon as a megaphone, our focus gets put on a single, unified voice—presumably God's voice. That voice is then said to be the one, clear voice speaking—not Moses or Matthew; not Peter or Paul. It's all God! This sounds like such a holy thing, and it's presented as a "high view of Scripture." The other voices in biblical texts are incidental; they are merely speaking what they have been given by the One voice. The result is that they all end up speaking a perfect harmony. The individual authors and their texts in the one, true, canon converge and coalesce—like multiple stacked chocolate bars melting into one another under the warm sun.

This approach sounds almost like the ancient letter of Aristeas (3rd or 2nd century BCE) which boasts 72 translators of the Hebrew texts into Greek over 72 days in 72 rooms, and all coming out with the same translation, presumably because God is *really* the one doing the translating. It's a *holy* idea. It *feels* divine. It's *presented* as a "high view" of Scripture.

But it's fiction.

A broad example of how canon is viewed as God's megaphone, in which the one voice of God essentially drowns out all others, is how the four gospels are routinely read in much or most contemporary Christianity. Essentially, they are seen as all telling different parts of the one story of Jesus. So choosing texts from one Gospel or another and placing them alongside the other is routine. In this way, the four gospels are forced to agree with each other to make them tell a homogenized, smooth and coherent story of Jesus. It is rare that the individual gospels are allowed to tell their own stories for their own reasons, or that tensions between the stories are allowed to stand.

Another example might be reading, say, 2Tim 3:15f and 2Pt 1:20f back to back, as if they are in the same context and written for the express purpose of providing biblical proof of inspiration and canonicity. They are also read through the protective shield of an overriding, already existing theory of inspiration that provides a new context for both texts so as to support the ruling theology.

There are many other examples, but the two just mentioned force a particular view of inspiration and canon over the texts. In doing so, the texts are coerced into complying with the overarching theology.

Kruger does exactly this. He presents *canon* as a holy, divine, pre-destined thing in itself, and he does this quite bluntly and openly on the basis of a theological platform. This move sounds like a good and holy thing: to honor and respect the Bible as the word of the sovereign God. And it is put forward as a simple and subtle "correction" to other approaches. But there is nothing subtle about it; the impact is more like a meteor strike that forever changes the landscape. Because now, the very concept of canon itself, including its extent and limits, is viewed as divinely inspired, not just the *texts* in the canon. This shifts the focus from *the texts* to *the canon*, as if by divine purpose; and it becomes a form of *canon veneration*, which is only a small step from bibliolatry.

We need to unmask this kind of *canon veneration*, to de-canonize it without demonizing the notion or existence of canon per se.

(b) We do far better to see canon as a conversation table where biblical authors bring their own stories, accounts, and arguments to the table through their individual texts. Like all specific stories, these *sacred texts* are diverse and multiform. They address different

70

issues to different people at different times in different locations for different reasons—and in different voices. And there is no question that on some matters, they stand in tension with each other. Is canon important? Of course it is! It provides a conversation table to bring varied authors together through their texts as conversation partners. *But the table is not the focus; the texts and their messages are the focus.* And in the midst of this, there is no "canonical necessity for compliance"; no need to paint them all with the same kind of theological brush to eliminate existing differences of details or perspective.

One of the best examples for why canon is better viewed as a conversation table is the fact that the four gospels were kept side by side instead of meshing them together and replacing them by something like the Diatessaron (a mid 2nd century Gospel harmony that blended all four gospels into one account, and which was used as the standard text [instead of the four gospels] into the fifth century in Syriac-speaking churches). Placing them side by side allows each of the four gospels to tell its own story from beginning to end, both allowing and generating conversation about the similarities and differences, but with no textual necessity of conflating accounts or resolving differences or discrepancies in details.

The same can be said for the competing creation accounts in Genesis 1, 2, and 3, and for the somewhat parallel accounts in Kings and Chronicles.

And as for texts like 2Tim 3:15f and 2Pt 1:20f, they're far better read separately and contextually, each making its own case, not as conflated statements or as contorted into defending a forthcoming New Testament canon. In this type of genuinely contextual reading, each is allowed, separately, to promote the beneficial nature of sacred, inspired texts (2Tim 3:15f), and the trustworthiness of prophetic texts (2Pt 1:20f), where such texts are known to both author and reader.

This kind of "conversation table" handling of biblical texts is extremely hard to do for anyone who views canon primarily as God's megaphone. There are many other examples, but those listed illustrate how to allow texts to stand on their own two feet without having to be propped up by a particular predetermined theology of canon or inspiration.

In the next chapter, I'll ask whether we are more canon-centric or text-centric as we think about canon. There is a difference.

—8—

Canon or Text Centric

Christianity is the world's largest religion, making up 31% (approximately 2.4 billion people) of the world's population.[72] During its history, Christianity has divided itself into a number of major populations:

Catholicism: 1.345 billion
Protestantism: 800 million to 1 billion
Eastern Orthodoxy: 220 million
Oriental Orthodoxy: 62 million
Non-trinitarian Restorationism: 60 million
Nestorianism: 0.6 million
(Others could be listed)

Since these groups hold several different specific canons,[73] one might wonder whether it is wise or even appropriate to have a

---

[72] The numbers may vary depending on terminology and sources. The numbers listed here are intended as illustrative rather than scientific, and are based on a Google generative AI search.

[73] Differences in canon have mostly to do with the limits of the Old Testament, but there are some differences also for the New Testament. The Ethiopian and Eritrean Orthodox Tewahedo Churches officially list 81 books (some sources claim 84 or 88) in their canon affecting both Old and New Testaments, making it the largest and most diversified biblical canon in worldwide Christianity. The additions in the New Testament help explain that the divine and human natures of Christ are considered as *tewahedo* ("united into one nature"), the only way human salvation is possible. A useful general comparison chart for the biblical canon can be seen in Wikipedia's article on "Biblical Canon." More

competitive or adversarial spirit about which Christian canon is "the *right* one." Although some might believe that the church has always had a single canon until the questions of recent times, quite the opposite is true. Worldwide Christianity has never, at any time, had a single, unified biblical canon.

As mentioned last chapter, unified canons have only existed within particular groups. Hence, the general approach among Christians has often been to view true Christianity and the right Bible from "where I stand, looking out." That way, my church and the Bible I use are the right ones, and if others differ, I might wonder why they want to change the Bible.

If you have followed the flow and arguments of this book, by now it should be clear that I am not offering an anti-canon statement. Canons can be extremely valuable. I am, rather, attempting to hold the terms *texts* and *canon* in sharp contradistinction to see what biblical and related texts say about them. At this point, I can now make two fairly pointed observations:

1. *Sacred texts* are clearly of major interest for both Jewish and Christian writers of the 1st century CE and before.

2. The concept of a *canon* of Old or New Testament books[74] cannot be demonstrated as even an *awareness* of either Jewish or Christian writers of that same period.

---

definitively, see the canon lists in the appendices of McDonald 2007, and the thorough lists in Gallagher/Mead 2017.

[74] As noted already, Kruger states flatly, "Yes, they already had an Old Testament canon," Kruger 2023, at 11:34. But he is just as flatly wrong. In chapter 2, I gave attention to Kruger's muddled and slippery use of the terms *authority* and *canon* in his speeches, despite that his "ontological definition" of canon is "what the canon is in and of itself, namely *the authoritative books that God gave his corporate church.*" Kruger 2013, 40, his italics. In actual practice, he has a specific list of books (a specific canon)F in mind.

The main issue for this chapter is whether it is best or appropriate to approach canon theoretically or functionally, and whether we are *canon-centric* or *text-centric*.[75] They are not the same.

1. Theoretical (Canon-Centric)

As noted especially in chapters 1 and 2 of this book, Kruger focuses on canon as the divine intention of God (he calls this the *ontological definition* of canon—what canon is in its essence). He thinks God appointed authors to write specific individual books that, as soon as the ink was dry, filled the slot of yet one more divinely intended piece of the predetermined canon. They were part of the canon whether anyone knew it or not.[76] Kruger asks some fine questions about whether anything in the 1st century led to a canon, or whether early Christians would have been open to new writings, or would have regarded some emerging Christian writings as "scripture," or whether early writers would have been aware that they carried some authority. But even if all of these are answered in the affirmative, not one of them proves a canon-consciousness in any New Testament writing. I have tried to demonstrate this in specific texts throughout this book.

Kruger offers a kind of "so many whiskers make a beard" argument, but his assertion that a book was part of the canon ten minutes after it was written, unfortunately (like the Letter of Aristeas), turns out to be fiction. About this, I have two comments:

---

[75] To be sure, Christians are to be God and Christ centered through the Holy Spirit, not either canon-centered or text-centered (cf. 2Corinthians 3; numerous Gospel texts, et al.). But the focus of this comparison is between these two.

[76] "The Gospel of John would have been 'canon' 10 minutes after it was written, but the early church would not yet have known it. It was only at a later point, when the corporate church had finally recognized which books belonged in the canon, that it could then look back and realize that there was a 'canon' even in the 1st century." Kruger 2013, 40, and fn 54.

First, Kruger's approach is theoretical, speculative, and hypothetical. It focuses on attributes of what a biblical canon is in the mind of God. And it looks very much like a reincarnation of Plato's perfect tree, where the *form* (the idea) is the real tree, and the visible tree is merely the *shadow* or changeable substance we see with our eyes. In this kind of current canon-talk, as represented in Kruger, the *idea* of canon is in God's mind (from creation), and the shadow is the imperfect, visible efforts at and current state of canon that exists in the imperfect, worldwide church today.

This approach also looks very much like (because it is related to it!) the argument for the New Testament's theoretical "original autographs"—none of which exist and which are singled out (by Kruger and many others) to be inerrant, meaning, for Kruger, true and without error.[77] Of course, manuscripts that do not exist can be said to be anything we like; so by definition, the approach is theoretical. With respect to canon, those (like Kruger) who focus on such topics have strained at all kinds of texts to show "what the Bible says, implies, or means" about canon, when our biblical texts actually say nothing at all about canon.[78] The problem is, such conclusions have, historically and often, worked their way into becoming so doctrinally entrenched, as to be almost the 4th person of the Godhead.[79]

Second, Kruger's approach is also canon-centric. This does not mean that he merely talks about canon, but that he puts *canon* (rather than *sacred texts*) at the center of attention.[80] He does this because he makes the two terms (*texts* and *canon*) imply each other, and then he reads his definition back into specific texts. This is a fundamental blunder; a procedural fallacy.

---

[77] See interview by Alisa Childers Kruger 2022.

[78] I've given numerous examples of this in chapters 1-5.

[79] One example is the Warfield/Kruger trajectory of thinking; another is the "Chicago Statement on Biblical Inerrancy." See also Brown 2022.

[80] The point, again, is about a comparison only of *text* focus with *canon* focus.

Once *canon* is seen as the same thing as, and is put in the place of, *sacred texts*, once it takes center stage, once theologies about that canon begin to subsume texts into the canon (i.e., to surpass, over-rule, and even sideline the texts within a particular view of canon[81]), the locus of hermeneutical attention and understanding moves from the *authors* of the texts to *interpreters* of some later date, near or far. This changes the understanding of texts, their intent, their message, and their value.

(And, by the way, this is exactly why, in Kruger's program, Jude simply cannot be allowed to be thinking of 1Enoch's prophecy as "sacred text," but as merely a "helpful book."[82])

Kruger's approach is presented as something like a "Quest for the Holy Canon" and as a high view of Scripture. In the process, it is so theoretical and canon-centric that it is almost a caricature of itself. It is built on a predetermined theological basis and on highly questionable interpretations of biblical texts to support the assertion that the one, true canon (which just happens to be the Protestant canon) was God's idea.[83]

In summary, Kruger's canon-centric approach to texts

1. assumes theoretically that the notion of canon is God's idea;

2. elevates the idea of a predestined, divinely chosen canon to the prominent position of attention and concern above and beyond specific, individual documents;

3. has canon take on a life of its own where it becomes its own new, self-contained, closed system for understaning and interpretation;

---

[81] This invariably happens with the gospels, but also can happen with any other text.

[82] Kruger 2023 Q&A at 15:40. See chapter 2 above.

[83] This has been demonstrated with specific texts throughout this book.

4. makes canon primarily function as God's pre-planned megaphone to the world; and

5. turns canon into an object of veneration.

There is certainly a sense that a canon of texts is *an authoritative collection* of texts for a given community, and that the totality of that canon can become more than the sum of its parts. But the question is whether a given Christian community focuses more on

1. *the authoritative **collection*** of texts (which implies there is only one right collection); or on

2. a collection of *authoritative **texts*** (which focuses on the contents of texts more than on which collection is right).

There is a difference. And Kruger pays homage on the first.

The problem is, the more canon-centric a community becomes, the more the canon (as a self-focused, idealized entity) in numerous ways begins to supersede, override, marginalize, flatten, or silence specific texts and the emphases within them. And the fundamental functions of texts begin to melt into concerns about the canon.

2. Functional (Text-Centric)

In contrast, a text-centric[84] view of canon can be represented like scrolls and manuscripts on a table. This view makes a distinction between the *documents* (i.e., the cherished or sacred texts that are accepted as authoritative), and the later constructed *table* that holds them. It is not the table they are placed on that is ultimately authoritative or the primary focus. That honor is reserved for the texts themselves.

---

[84] I repeat that *text-centric* means, here, a focus on texts and documents that are viewed as authoritative texts, rather than on canon for its own sake.

There is a very subtle, but quite significant, distinction between a *table of authoritative books*, as opposed to *an authoritative table of books*. It is not the particular table that is primary, but the books placed on the table.

In this way, a canon may be described as a kind of *conversation table* that respects the individual voices (texts) that have gathered around it. Rather than co-opt those texts into an alternate "canon universe" or "canon context," such a view of canon allows its individual documents to speak to their original, specific recipients at specific times for specific reasons, while also (at one time or another) coming into conversation with other documents. In this way, canon is more properly seen in its natural, functional role of bringing disparate authoritative texts together into association with one another. And this encourages a focused, whole-hearted, energetic pursuit of conversation with God through said sacred texts, where the focus is on the contents of the sacred texts themselves, and not on some imagined pre-planned canon. This latter notion of a pre-planned canon comes along only at a later stage of development.

That is why it is necessary to carefully consider the specific claims within biblical texts:

1. that it is *sacred texts themselves* that are said to be "inspired of God";[85]

2. that it is *prophecies* from God that are spoken by "those carried along by the Holy Spirit";

3. and that there is no promise, or indication, or even a hint that a single, once-for-all, canon was God's great divine secret, hidden, but now in the process of coming to light.

---

[85] Clarify-----Because some will improperly object that it is only Scripture that is said to be inspired, I refer again to Collier 2024 for both of these texts and for the study as a whole.

Canon:

a Table of
Authoritative
Books?

OR

an Authoritative
Table of
Books?

Looking at canon as a naturally developing, after-the-fact *conversation table* is a useful corrective. It places the emphasis and focus where it belongs:

> on the *texts* themselves (as holy and sacred texts),

> rather than on a *canon* per se (as if it were the single, once-for-all, divinely planned, predestined form or template for what "the canon" was supposed to look like in its ideal state).

In this way, the emphasis is placed squarely on how earlier, relatively independent *sacred texts* arise and begin to perform authoritatively within communities as those texts have walked along the path (like Jesus on the road to Emmaus) with people of faith.

The fact that they might be on some kind of natural trajectory toward an eventual full-blown canon of one shape or another does not imply that this is an out-of-the-ordinary development. Otherwise, how does one explain the eventual emergence of multiple canons within related but divergent communities of faith? The very fact that a number of Christian canons *did* emerge out of the Jewish and Christian texts is not at all an aberrant thing, nor should it be a surprise. And the key to understanding this is the inherent *ontology* of canon, i.e., the essence of canon—what it is, in and of itself. This ontology or essence is not a superimposed theory or philosophical view, but an inherently *functional* (i.e., operational, active) process.

I'll now flesh out this view of canon.

—9—

The Essence of Canon

The ontology of a biblical canon, in its essence, is functional. This amounts to a rejection of Kruger's central contention; namely, that the ontology of canon is a pre-formed idea in the mind of God. A biblical canon is, rather, a normal extension of communities of faith that produce sacred literature; and such a canon's primary purpose is functional—to bring sacred texts together for a community's sake. And in every case, the focus is not on the canon per se, but on the sacred texts within the particular canon.

1. Act of Faith

So now, I will offer a functional definition or description of a biblical canon that is at once functionally sensitive, historically authentic, and fully respectful of biblical texts.

The description I now offer will attempt to be simple, yet precise; to deal faithfully and carefully with the sacred texts we have in front of us; to make a positive case, without overstating it; and to clearly acknowledge (and celebrate!) the continuing work of God in the church throughout the world, rather than only within particular denominational borders. Here it is:

A biblical canon[86]
—whether ancient or modern,
whether Catholic, Orthodox, Protestant, or other—
is in essence
an act of faith, by communities of faith,
in search of an ongoing conversation with God
through texts deemed holy and sacred.

Adopted as a sweeping or overarching portrayal of "what canon is"(in the visible world), this outlook can breathe new life into the way we view, understand, and apply biblical texts in everyday circumstances.

2. Eminent Truths

This not only does not diminish the Bible in any way, it, in fact, helps us affirm three eminent truths about canon:

a. God still working

The first eminent truth: *God is still at work through the church world-wide as that church keeps on seeking conversation with God through holy texts!* This is not about having or owning a holy book we can hold up as a trophy and call it, as in a Pinocchio syndrome, *the real Bible;* it's rather about engaging the authors of ancient and sacred texts on the most important questions of life and existence. And, through them, engaging God in continual conversation.

---

[86] There are, of course, such things as non-biblical canons. As examples, the Quranic canon and, more generally, the Western Canon or a literary canon. Buddhism has multiple canons in multiple languages. Not all religions have canons or even sacred texts for passing on their tenets: e.g., Hinduism and Shintoism. The *Population Education* website notes that, "While there are around 10,000 distinct religions in the world, over three-quarters of the global population adheres to one of these four—Christianity (31%), Islam (24%), Hinduism (15%), and Buddhism (7%). "
https://populationeducation.org/world-population-by-religion-a-global-tapestry-of-faith/, accessed 6/11/2024.

b. Texts self-adapting

The second eminent truth: *The proliferation and applications of sacred texts through biblical authors (including the priests, the prophets, the apostles, and even Jesus himself, although not an author)—they all model for us the* **adaptability** *of sacred ideas and texts for ever new times, places, and situations!*

By *self-adapting*, I do not mean at all what Kruger means by "self-authenticating," which I critiqued in chapter 1. I myself am referring to how biblical writers were in constant conversation with previous authors and texts, and because of that, they are continually adapting previous theological ideas in new, creative, and relevant ways. While popular Christianity often fixates on the unchangeable nature of God and what is thought to be God's divine plan (as that plan is variously laid out by diverse theological systems), the intricacies of ancient texts themselves bear witness *against* any kind of stagnation, and move *into* an incredible and diverse world of conversation taking place back and forth over the span of centuries. Biblical authors engage each other, challenge their own readers, and model for us how to engage current understandings and previous ideas. So it's not only OK for us to challenge particular Christian views about our holy texts, it is exactly what we are taught to do by those authors through their texts. Just because we challenge particular *views* about the Bible we think might be inadequate, outdated, or improper, does not mean we are attacking our ancient, *sacred texts*.

c. Canon naturally emerging

The third eminent truth is that *Canon is a natural, functional extension from within communities that produce written texts.* It happens naturally and over time within communities of faith and purpose. Canon is one way that communities evaluate and organize important beliefs, teachings, and texts that may, in fact, become sacred for them. Canons not only emerge naturally from, but are essential to communities of faith and purpose, to nurture, shape, and guide them. The relationship between canon and community is very much a symbiotic relationship. A reciprocal relationship.

3. Canon as Conversation

And so, now, for the kicker, and this part is crucial! Why crucial? Because some people get scared and jump to the conclusion that God is getting left out of my description, here—that unless we say all the same old tired, traditional words that do not occur anywhere in our sacred texts (words like *inerrant*, or *infallible*, or that God planned the canon—almost to the effect that God wrote the Bible and dropped it out of heaven) that we are somehow denying the inspiration of our sacred texts. But that is simply false.

So, then, here's the kicker. If we truly believe that God is active in the community of faith—if it is not merely lip-service that we give to this notion—then are we not compelled to see and understand that

**a biblical canon
is the vital and outworking act of faith,
by communities of faith,
as they search—diligently—
for an ongoing conversation with God,
through the texts they have received
as sacred!**

This functional definition or description of canon, if understood and taken to heart, is nothing less than the expression that God is at work in our communities of faith.

- It could help transform how Bible readers not only view the Bible more dynamically, but how they apply it more energetically to the challenges, questions, and situations of everyday life. Because, that is how its texts were written!

- It could help to bring about incredibly powerful works in our communities of faith.

- It could help set us free, as Christian readers, from constraining, theoretical views—views which do not actually fit with the contents of our biblical texts.

- It could fundamentally change the terms and conditions of conclusions that are based more in contrived doctrinal arguments than in a careful examination of biblical texts.

- It could also provide a better footing for a reasonable discussion about the value of the Bible in our rapidly changing times.

With these thoughts about what a new paradigm for approaching canon might look like, I turn finally to ask, "What is the focus of our faith?"

−10−

The Focus of Our Faith

As members of diverse Christian communities, there is no reason that we should have a competitive or adversarial spirit about canon. The undeniable fact is that Christians worldwide have somewhat different canons (to whatever degree) and many different traditions! Hence, the Canon Wars are unnecessary and should come to an end.

Do we really think, after all of this time, that God is expecting the Christians of the world to adopt a single canon—namely, ours?! Or that we, alone, are the ones who have chosen the one, true and right canon? The canon God thought up as *the divine idea* before the foundation of the world? And that all other Christians are just wrong?

Perhaps we should consider the arrogance—perhaps the audacity—of such a path. Or the insanity of it!

The center of our Christian faith is not that there is only one particular canon; nor is the center made up of the boundaries of our canons or the edges of our traditions. It's not even a New Testament canon over an Old Testament canon. From a Christian perspective, the center of faith is, rather, how God in Christ offers real and ultimate hope for humanity! This is where we should be spending our time and attentions.

So, as did our fore-parents for many generations (even though we might disagree with them on many or a few things), we should continue to act in faith, while seeking conversation with God through the multitude of texts that are available, many of which have now been collected—over centuries—into various, what we now call, *canons* of sacred texts.

Surely, we have more to celebrate from all of the texts, and more to learn from the mutual existence of such collections, than, in tribal fashion, to pit them against each other, just so we can boast in our notion that "There can be only one—and we have it!"[87]

The question is not, "Which canon is right?" Nor is it, "Which books belong in the one and only canon?" The question—the most *important* question about biblical texts facing the church to-day—is rather, "How do we take 2,000+ year old *texts* (found in whichever canon we choose), and bring them to bear on the lives of individuals, communities of faith, and nations today? How do we interact with the *sacred texts* that are in the collected canons of the world? How do we put these *holy texts* to work in ourselves and in the church-at-large throughout the world?"

Such a dynamic perspective about canon—an understanding of the difference between the terms *scripture* and *canon*, the terms *texts* and *canon*, and the concepts of a *theoretical* and *functional* view of canon—these can all make a difference in how we imagine, approach, and apply our precious biblical texts. Such an effort is well worth our time and attention.

---

[87] Or like some old, low-budget martial arts film in which the fighters taunt each other that "My kung-fu is better than yours!"

Part III
End Matter

Materials Quoted

My response to Kruger's video has included some of his written material as that helped to fill out some of the issues addressed, but it has not intended to be a full response to every aspect of that material. The following resources are listed because they came up at various stages of my response.

Personally, I recommend McDonald's approach and materials as the most helpful of all available today. Certainly, McDonald has written far more than I have listed below. I make no claims that he or anyone else would agree with any of my positions. [88]

Bauckham 1983	Bauckham, Richard J. *Jude, 2Peter*. Word Biblical Commentary, 1983.
Bird & Wright 2019	Bird, Michael; and Wright, N. T. *The New Testament in Its World*. SPCK and Zondervan Academic, 2019.
Brown 1997	Brown, Raymond. *An Introduction to the New Testament*. Doubleday, 1997.
Brown 2022	Brown, Derek J. "Updating the Chicago Statement on Biblical Inerrancy: A Proposal." Online *TGC* (*The Gospel Coalition*) March 15, 2022. https://www.thegospelcoalition.org/article/updating-chicago-statement/ Accessed 5/31/2024.
Chapman 2012	Chapman, S. B. "Second Temple Jewish Hermeneutics: How Canon is Not an Anachronism." In J. Ulrich, A. Jacobsen, & D. Brakke (Eds.). *Invention, Rewriting, Usurpation: Discursive Fights over Religious Traditions in Antiquity* (pp. 281–296). Frankfurt: Peter Lang, 2012.

---

[88] When I wrote *Scripture, Canon, & Inspiration* (2012), the topic was becoming popular, but not anything like it is now. There are many books on the topic. Kruger's books were coming out during the same time of my writing: 2010 (with Köstenberger), 2012, and 2013. I referred to the first of these in my book and gave a few paragraphs of critique. Kruger's books have risen as among the favorites defending and reviving a more traditional and conservative view. His 2023 speech that I've reviewed in this book are consistent with and grow out of his books. As I have indicated in throughout this book, I do not recommend Kruger's treatment of the topic. Rather, I highly recommend the numerous works of Lee Martin McDonald as the best single source on the topic.

Collier 2012	Collier, Gary D. *Scripture, Canon, & Inspiration*. Dialogē Press, 2012.
Collier 2024	Collier, Gary D. *Graphē in Biblical and Related Literature: Is the Term Scripture an Appropriate Translation in English Bibles?* 2nd Edition. Dialogē Press, 2024.
Evans 2005	Evans, Craig A. *Ancient Texts for New Testament Studies*. Hendrickson, 2005.
Fee 1995	Fee, Gordon. *1 and 2 Timothy and Titus*. New International Biblical Commentary. Hendrickson, 1995.
Gallagher/Mead 2017	Gallagher, Emon L. and Mead, John D. *The Biblical Canon Lists from Early Christianity*. Oxford, 2017.
Hagner 2012	Hagner, Donald. *The New Testament: A Historical and Theological Introduction*. Baker Academic, 2012.
Köstenberger 2010	Köstenberger, Andreas, and Kruger, Michael J. *The Heresy of Orthodoxy*. Crossway, 2010.
Kruger 2012	Kruger, Michael L. *Canon Revisited*. Crossway, 2012.
Kruger 2013	Kruger, Michael L. *The Question of Canon*. IVP, 2013.
Kruger 2022	Kruger, Michael L. "How do we make sense of textual variations with the doctrine of inerrancy?" Interviewed by Alisa Childers. https://www.youtube.com/watch?v=wcUyrZ9qUsU. Accessed 5/31/2024.
Kruger 2023	Kruger, Michael L. "7 Misconceptions about the Biblical Canon" (Under the title of "How We God the Bible") https://www.youtube.com/watch?v=vPUBjRxDQXo Feb 19, 2023.
Kruger 2023 Q&A	Kruger, Michael L. "Live Q&A" (Under the title of "Canon Q&A | Michael Kruger") https://www.youtube.com/watch?v=5MPb8gFsLNE Feb 19, 2023.
McDonald/Sanders 2002	McDonald, Lee Martin; Sanders, J. A. "Introduction." *The Canon Debate*. Hendrickson, 2002.
McDonald 2007	McDonald, Lee Martin. *The Biblical Canon*. Hendrickson, 2007.
McDonald 2020	McDonald, Lee Martin. "Fluidity in the Early Formation of the Hebrew Bible." *Hebrew Studies* 61 (2020): 73–96. https://www.jstor.org/stable/26950401.
O'Malley 2013	O'Malley, John W. *Trent: What Happened at the Council*. Belknap Press (Harvard), 2013.
Pfeiffer 1968	Pfeiffer, Rudolf. *History of Classical Scholarship from the Beginnings to the End of the Hellenistic Age*. Clarendon Press, 1968.
Roberts 1983	Roberts, Colin H.; Skeat, T. C. *The Birth of the Codex*. Oxford, 1983.
Tenney 1953	Tenney, Merrill. *New Testament Survey*. Eerdmans, 1953.

Materials Quoted

Warfield 1948

Warfield, B. B. (d. 1902) his book, *Inspiration and Authority of the Bible,* was published posthumously by Samuel G. Craig in 1948. The article on "Canon of the New Testament" (included as an appendix in the book) was published in 1892 by the American Sunday School Union.
Accessed 8/5/2024 through http://library.logcol-legepress.com/Craig%2C+Samuel+G.%2C+Fore-word+to+B.B.+Warfield%2C+The+Inspiration+and+Author-ity+of+the+Bible.pdf

Watson 2019

Watson, Francis. "The Canon and the Codex: On the Material Form of the Christian Bible" in *The Life of Texts: Evidence in Textual Production, Transmission, and Reception.* London: Bloomsbury Academic, 2019, 48-61, 208-210.

Index of Texts Noted

Abbreviations

JOSEPHUS

APOSTOLIC FATHERS

General Index

Abbreviations

BIBLICAL DOCUMENTS

Gen	1, 2Chr	Jer	Nah	Ac	Phlm
Ex	Ezra	Lam	Hab	Rom	Heb
Lev	Neh	Ezek	Zeph	1, 2Cor	Jas
Num	Esth	Dan	Hag	Gal	1, 2Pt
Deut	Job	Hos	Zech	Eph	1, 2, 3Jn
Josh	Ps (Pss)	Joel	Mal	Phil	Jude
Judg	Prov	Amos	Mt	Col	Rev
Ruth	Eccl	Obad	Mk	1, 2Th	
1, 2Sam	Song	Jonah	Lk	1, 2Tim	
1, 2Kgs	Isa	Mic	Jn	Titus	

OLD TESTAMENT APOCRYPHA

1-4Macc	1Maccabees	Sus	Susanna
Jdt	Judith	Tob	Tobit
Sir	Sirach (Ecclesiasticus)	Wis	Wisdom

APOCRYPHA & PSEUDEPIGRAPHA

1En.	1Enoch (Ethiopic Apocalypse)	TLev.	Testament of Levi
AEJ	Aristeas the Exegete	TMO	The Testament of Moses
APS	Apocalypse of Sedrach	TNap.	Testament of Naphtali
Aris.	Letter of Aristeas	TSim.	Testament of Simeon
ELD	Eldad and Modad	TZeb.	Testament of Zebulun
LIV	Lives of the Prophets		

JOSEPHUS

Apion	Against Apion
Ant.	Jewish Antiquities

PHILO OF ALEXANDRIA

Aet.	De aeternitate mundi	Ios.	De Iosepho
Agr.	De agricultura	Leg. 1-3	Legum allegoriae I, II, III
Conf.	De confusione linguarum	Mos. 1-2	De vita Mosis I, II
Decal.	De decalogo	Post.	De posteritate Caini
Det.	Quod deterius potiori insidari soleat	Prob.	Quod omnis probus liber sit
Ebr.	De ebrietate	Sacr.	De sacrificiis Abelis et Caini
Fug.	De fuga et inventione	Somn. 1-2	De somniis I, II
Gig.	De gigantibus	Spec. 1-4	De specialibus legibus I-IV
Her.	Quis rerum divinarum heres sit	Virt.	De virtutibus

Abbreviations

APOSTOLIC FATHERS

Barn.	*Barnabas*	Ign. *Eph.*	Ignatius, *To the Ephesians*
1–2 Cl.	*1–2 Clement*		
Did.	*Didache*		
Herm. *Vis.*	Shepherd Hermas, *Vision*		

EUSEBIUS

EH	*Ecclesiastical History*

Notes

Notes

Author

GARY D. COLLIER

B.A., MDiv., Th.M., Ph.D.
Biblical Literature & Languages

Director of
*The Institute for the Art of
Biblical Conversation
(IABC)*

Author of a growing list of books, most notably:

2024: *Canon Wars: Whose Idea Was the Biblical Canon? (A Response to Michael J. Kruger's "7 Misconceptions" about the Biblical Canon)*

2024: *Γραφή | graphē in Biblical and Related Literature: Is the Term "Scripture" an Appropriate Translation in English Bibles?*

2023: *I, Paulos: Shades of Conversation in 1 Thessalonians*

2021: *The Art of Biblical Conversation*

2019: *Scribes Trained for the Kingdom: A Pre-Grammar for New Testament Greek as a Spiritual Discipline*

2012: *Scripture, Canon, & Inspiration*

1993: *The Forgotten Treasure: Reading the Bible Like Jesus*

Complete author profile:
https://www.biblicalconversation.com/profile-gcollier

www.ingramcontent.com/pod-product-compliance
Lightning Source LLC
Chambersburg PA
CBHW051215120626
46547CB00013B/1362